THE JAGGED JOURNEY

CHUCK CRUMPTON

CEO – MEDPOINT, LLC

THE JAGGED JOURNEY

A Real Memoir about the Non-Perfect Path of
Life & Business

Advantage®

Published by Advantage, Charleston, South Carolina.
Member of Advantage Media Group.

ADVANTAGE is a registered trademark, and the Advantage colophon is a trademark of Advantage Media Group, Inc.

Printed in the United States of America.

10 9 8 7 6 5 4 3 2 1

ISBN: 978-1-64225-113-5
LCCN: 2019915819

Cover design by Jamie Wise.
Layout design by Wesley Strickland.

This publication is designed to provide accurate and authoritative information in regard to the subject matter covered. It is sold with the understanding that the publisher is not engaged in rendering legal, accounting, or other professional services. If legal advice or other expert assistance is required, the services of a competent professional person should be sought.

Advantage Media Group is proud to be a part of the Tree Neutral® program. Tree Neutral offsets the number of trees consumed in the production and printing of this book by taking proactive steps such as planting trees in direct proportion to the number of trees used to print books. To learn more about Tree Neutral, please visit **www.treeneutral. com.**

Advantage Media Group is a publisher of business, self-improvement, and professional development books and online learning. We help entrepreneurs, business leaders, and professionals share their Stories, Passion, and Knowledge to help others Learn & Grow. Do you have a manuscript or book idea that you would like us to consider for publishing? Please visit advantagefamily.com or call 1.866.775.1696.

Dedicated to my mom and dad, Charles and Linda Crumpton,
my heroes who have loved me unconditionally.

CONTENTS

PREFACE

I am not a writer.

When my doctor and good friend Dave Albenberg, MD, suggested I write a book "to tell my story," I laughed out loud. I can't begin to tell you how daunting I perceived the process of writing a book could be. Without his words of encouragement and countless hours of listening to the pain points of my journey, I would not have attempted this project in a million years. Thank you, Dave, for being a great doctor and even better friend.

With careful diligence over each of the thirty-five thousand words of this book, I'm recounting my life and journey with what I believe is 100 percent accurate recall—a process that took nearly a year from the time I put pen to paper until the physical book was in hand. I'm very appreciative of my incredible leadership team at Medpoint LLC for giving me the time and latitude while I tackled the task of writing. A big thanks to my publishing team, especially Regina, my project editor, who listened and coached me for hours and hours as I unpacked over fifty years of life and business. I have equated the process of writing this book to something like driving the little boat in the amusement park. You may think you're driving the vessel around the lake, with fierce turns to the right and left, but really, it's the track under the boat that keeps you on target and safe.

In the pages ahead, I've attempted to honor and thank a handful of people, but time and word count will prevent me from being exhaustive with that list. There are just too many people whom I owe gratitude to and who have been on this roller-coaster journey with me to do it justice.

I had three major goals in writing this book:

1. To honor my mom and dad. Their unconditional love has sustained and astonished me for fifty-six years.

2. To leave a positive and memorable item of perpetuity for Katie and Charles, the greatest gifts in life a dad could ever ask for.

3. To encourage everyone, whether on the mountain or down in the valley, with real, raw, and transparent talk through actual life events.

I hope in some small way this book helps you be a better partner, friend, parent, mentor, and leader.

Chuck

CHAPTER 1

NOT WHAT I EXPECTED

Easter morning, 2014. I found myself sitting alone in my recently rented apartment where I had only a folding table and chair, a wineglass, a television, and a bed. It was a stark contrast to where I had been for fifteen years prior. There I sat, on that early spring morning, not really knowing how I ended up there after what I thought was a perfect path of building my career, building a home, building my family.

The night before, for the last time, I left the home where my wife and I had raised two children. That was the last day of a twenty-eight-year marriage that was ending in divorce.

At eleven thirty the night before, I got into a cab and rode away from that home, with most of my clothes thrown quickly together in trash bags. My marriage and my home, my refuge, had become toxic and unhealthy. We had tried years of counseling to no avail. I'm an advocate of counseling—I even sat on the board of a counseling company—but my marriage had deteriorated too far to come back to a healthy point. Andrew Franssen, our counselor, was truly amazing, insightful, and humbly authentic, but it was just too late.

Riding in the darkness, I was lost in my thoughts until the cabdriver broke the silence with some words of wisdom and comfort I will never forget. "You know, things look bad, and they probably will get worse," he said. "But things will get better. You will be a happier person."

I was too numb to do more than stare back at him and nod. A little after midnight, we pulled up in front of the apartment building. The driver helped me to my door, carrying my bags of clothes into the room and placing them on the living room floor.

The next morning, when I saw the trash bags in the middle of the floor, all I could think was, *How did I end up here? This is not what I expected.*

BUILDING A LIFE

For the first few days in my new "home," I just sat there on that folding chair, staring at a blank wall and a muted TV, just trying to figure out where to go from here.

The home I had left behind was the sixth in a series of progressively larger, more spectacular homes that had mirrored my growing career. It was a magnificent 5,200-square-foot house that had been meticulously designed and custom built by Jon Peery. Every angle, every inch contained some detail that I had planned and worked through with the builder and architect.

It was also a place where I had built a lot of memories with my family.

My son, Charles, was age five when construction on the home began. He and I actually started the project by clearing the ten-acre country property ourselves. I used a chain saw to cut down trees in a circular fashion, and together, we created the clearing for what would ultimately be the homesite.

It took a year to have the home built, and during that time, my son and I would go out in the woods and play cowboys and Indians, with my son dressed up in his cowboy hat and boots. Even after the house was built, we spent a lot of time playing on the property and in the woods. My son and I also did a lot of target and skeet shooting on the sprawling ten acres. And it was the ideal place for hours-long games of paintball with our best friends.

For his eighth birthday, my son told me he wanted a tree house. I hired a contractor to come out and construct it twenty-five feet up in one of the trees in the woods. The contractor worked nights and weekends to put the tree house together, and in between, I carried the lumber to the site. Every couple of days, we would go drive a few nails as our part in the project, but to my young son, it seemed like we were building it together. "Daddy, we're really making good progress on this," he'd say. The contractor and I finished the tree house at ten o'clock the night before my son's birthday, and we celebrated in the tree house the next day, twenty-five feet aboveground.

As part of the customization of the home, I also had a basketball court built for my daughter, Katie—a basketball phenom—and she and I spent hours and hours shooting hoops together.

The backyard also had a very large, twenty-by-forty, in-ground, twenty-eight-thousand-gallon pool with Italian stone and a huge deck with a hot tub. We had a lot of parties and birthday events around that pool, and I remember my son spending many Sunday afternoons swimming after a nap.

Holidays were especially fun in the house. To further convince my kids that there really was a Santa Claus, I bought a Santa suit and then made an agreement with my neighbors: if they would dress up as Santa for my kids, I would do the same for theirs. On Christmas Eve, I'd lie down on the bed upstairs with my kids, and on cue, a neighbor would enter the living room downstairs, wearing the suit, shaking jingle bells, and chanting, "Ho, ho, ho." When we heard that Santa was in the house, I'd lay my arm over my son to steady him, and I would feel his heart beating out of his chest from the excitement.

We hosted many visitors and entertained often in that house. We welcomed foreign-born students from China and Germany, having them as guests while they attended area schools. We also had friends and family over for epic Super Bowl parties. The entire third floor was a sports room with a massive TV and surround sound, and as many as eighty-five people showed up for the game.

One of the most difficult memories I still struggle with is the wall along the stairwell going up to the third floor. Everyone who passed that wall was invited to write a message. When I left the house, it was covered with fifteen years of messages written by friends, family, and neighbors—loved ones from all over the world.

Although that part of my life's journey ended very painfully, the memories I made with my kids, family, and friends, inside and outside that house, will last forever.

YOU ARE FREE

Sitting there in that empty apartment in Greenville, South Carolina, I began to slowly get some perspective. As my head began to clear, it dawned on me one day that I had another option for living arrangements.

A year earlier, when my son was a senior in high school, I had bought a house four hours to the southeast, in Charleston. He was going to the College of Charleston, and instead of paying rent for him at one of the dormitories, I bought the house for him to stay in, and for its investment value. But after a year in Charleston, he decided to transfer to college in San Diego.

Since he was no longer occupying the house, I thought, *Why am I paying rent on this short-term-lease apartment when I have a house being vacated in Charleston?* I considered staying in the apartment and renting out the Charleston house. Then I realized that living in Charleston would give me some healthy distance from the painful memories. It would give me some space to heal.

The first week I was in the Charleston house alone, I went outside to get some fresh air with a cold martini and noticed some faded graffiti scrawled across a brick wall in front of my neighbor's house. I stood back to read what was written and realized that it was three words.

You are free

Those three words grabbed me by the heart. As I stood there looking at them, I knew that God had put those three words there for me. Yes, they were really the work of an anonymous writer, written no telling how many years ago, but I felt in my heart that those words were meant for me.

Those three words spurred me on as I began to get my life back in order.

BEGINNING TO HEAL

Just as I had in my "past life," I began to focus on building a new home—this time, for myself.

When I first moved in after my son and his two buddies had vacated the property, it reminded me of a fraternity house. The walls were covered with posters of Clint Eastwood and Jack Daniel's, and there was a neon Bud Light sign in the kitchen.

Again, I thought, *This is not what I expected at this point in my life.*

I slowly began to change the decor in the Charleston house. One room at a time, and with the help of friends, I turned it into a quintessential Charleston home with Old South decorations and furniture. For a time there, living in a half-frat-house, half-Old-South home, I think my friends might have had some concerns about my mental state.

Over time, that one-hundred-year-old house began to metamorphose into a place more suitable for a fifty-year-old.

Still, the days and nights were long and lonely.

Initially as a way of socializing again, I decided to turn part of the Charleston home into an Airbnb. I placed my ad on the Airbnb website, and within forty-five minutes I had my first reservation. It was the first of eighty-five reservations I would have over the next year.

People from across the United States and all over the world—Denmark, Switzerland, England, Hong Kong—came to stay with me in the house. Having other people in the house gave me someone to talk to, a way to occupy my mind. But nearly every one of those reservations meant a new, phenomenal story. And listening to their stories, learning about their lives, turned out to be great therapy.

One of the families that stayed with me had a five-year-old daughter, Savannah, who, after a day of sightseeing, would ask her parents, "Can I sit with Mr. Chuck on the couch?" She would sit there next to me, coloring or playing a video game. When the family left, she gave me a Valentine's heart, a small handmade card that read, "Mr. Chuck, I love you." I still have that card to this day; it reminds me of some of the gifts my daughter made for me when she was growing up.

Then there was four-foot-nine, eighty-three-year-old Trudy, who had a daughter roughly my age and a granddaughter about my daughter's age. They came from Vermont and stayed during a cold, rainy February. Late one Sunday afternoon, Trudy joined us for a Bloody Mary and conversation. After we finished the first drink, I got up to fix another for myself, and when I asked her if she'd like one more, she said, "Yes, but make mine stronger." I adored her spunk.

And then there was Nathan, a young, single guy in his late twenties who came from Texas to interview with a Charleston company. Although I'm a North Carolina Tar Heels fan, and he's a fan of the bad guys, the Duke Blue Devils, I didn't hold that against him. He got the job in Charleston, and we're still very close friends. In fact, he invited us to his wedding in France last fall.

In some ways, I was rebuilding the friendship wall that had graced my family's stairwell in Greenville. I put out a guest book at the Charleston house, and everyone who stayed with me made an entry in it. I had wonderful reviews, and I still have friendships with some of my Airbnb guests.

Building out my friendship network in Charleston also meant hitting a neighborhood restaurant, Halls Chophouse, a couple of nights a week. There, Billy Hall, the owner's son, would greet me with a hug and a hearty "Welcome to Halls." Since it was within walking distance, on days that I could only manage a mental shower and getting dressed up, I could scoot out the door of my house and head over to Halls, and they'd know exactly what I wanted without me even looking at a menu. It was a safe place for me to heal because they made me feel like a familiar friend. After a nice meal, a glass of wine, some friendly banter, and a little TV, I would scoot out the back door and head for home.

WORKING IT OUT

As I healed from the divorce, I continued to work in Greenville, at the office of the successful healthcare consulting company that I had built, Medpoint LLC. I had started the company in the toolshed of my garage in 2002. The company was growing year over year, and we had reached several million in revenue after twelve years in business—a huge success that came with the sacrifice of family and our employees/consultants around the world.

It was a four-hour commute from Charleston to Greenville, one marked by a deep pain every time I crossed the county line. My heart sank to the point of being physically ill whenever I saw the Greenville County road sign because it resonated with me as a place of failure.

The truth is, I don't know what would have happened had it not been for the Medpoint senior management team—Renee, Rich, Danna, and Rachel. There were days that I could not get out of bed, much less make it to work. The days that I did show up, I could usually only manage about an hour or two of work.

But those four senior leaders kept the company going and even grew it during my mental and physical absence. The company had a large payroll and a lot of financial responsibility. But those four stepped it up and led the business every day, every week, every quarter. Their diligence and dedication—and their love and passion for not only me but for our business and all the one hundred-plus people and their families who supported the business—gave me the time I needed to heal.

That allowed me to sit in an apartment with no pictures, or later to sit in my backyard or on the beach and just try to figure life out. I will forever be grateful to them for running the business and carrying me through some of the darkest hours of my twenty-five-year career.

A NEW CLOSENESS

Thankfully, in addition to the support of my senior management team, I also had others who were there for me. As my foundation, my parents, my brother, and my children were all there for me, supporting me unconditionally with phone calls and prayers, and sometimes tears. On some level, I think I was going through some form of post-traumatic stress disorder (PTSD).

If it was possible to do so, I think I became even more focused on my children. I developed a closeness with them that I never had up to that point. We transitioned from a father/children relationship to being father/children/friends. Part of that began when I had to sit down with them one day and tell them the hardcore truth about the marriage coming to an end. Those were difficult conversations, but they took our transparency to a whole other level. They were appropriately privy to everything because I wanted nothing to be hidden. At the same time, I worked very hard to honor their mother and not be disparaging, as can be the case in difficult divorces. Admittedly, that's been difficult at times, but I'm trying to make everything as easy as I can on what is now our fragmented family.

For the first time during the divorce years, so many of the people closest to me began to see me as a normal person. Instead of being someone for whom every job was better, every house was bigger, every car was nicer, I became broken and vulnerable. That allowed others to feel safe in opening up and sharing with me. My brother told me things I had never known about him. My daughter revealed some of her closest-guarded secrets to me, something she probably would have never been able to do had I been the hard-ass, stalwart, successful dad and business owner that I had portrayed myself as being all the years prior. When we strip away all the facade and we live life transparently and vulnerably, that's when people get into our life and our world.

While my divorce was a great failure for me, it opened up some of the most beautiful relationships I could have ever imagined in my life. During the four years that it took for the divorce to become final, I had some of the most transparent conversations that I've ever enjoyed.

It's been said, "When a window closes, a door opens. But the hallway may suck." When that window of my marriage closed, and the door to my new life opened, the hallway definitely sucked. But it brought about some beautiful relationships as a result.

What I've discovered is that life is not compartmentalized. The marriage and divorce affected my whole life; it still affects me and those that I love today.

But I'm sharing with you my story in part because I want you to know that no matter where you are in your life, you're not alone. If you let people in, if you let people love you, there will always be someone to walk that dark journey with you. But you've got to let them in.

After four years of darkness and healing, I remember vividly the day my divorce was final. I was on my way to Greenville when I got a call that a settlement had been reached. "We have an appointment with the judge at noon to sign the final divorce decree," my attorney said. I was forty-five minutes away, just enough time to get there and change into the suit I had in the trunk of my car. When I arrived at his offices, I ran into a restroom and put on the suit, and then together, he and I drove to the courthouse to appear before the judge. After only fifteen minutes, my twenty-eight-year marriage was over.

It was a day of unbelievable sadness at the close of one chapter of my life, but it also came with an unbelievable feeling of freedom at a new chapter before me.

CHAPTER 2

TOBACCO ROAD

My life's journey started in a far different place than where I am today, but along the way, I learned many lessons and made many friends whom I still hold near and dear.

I was born in May 1963 on a tobacco farm in Blanch, North Carolina, less than an hour from the home of my beloved University of North Carolina (UNC) Tar Heels. The farm was in Caswell County, a rural agricultural community about seven miles from the county seat. It was a community filled with 22,646 good people who cared about each other; growing up, it seemed like I attended the weddings and funerals of every family in the county. I have been forever grateful for wonderful families and friends like the Daniels, Kirbys, Tatums, and Blalocks who have cared so deeply for my family all these years. These are just a few—so many more should be recognized.

My parents, Charles and Linda Crumpton, are the best of people, the best of parents. They have been married for nearly sixty years as I write this book, and they have loved me unconditionally. My brother, David, is a model of strong heart and unwavering loyalty, and every day, I am so thankful that he survived a horrific motorcycle accident at age nine and went on to lead a beautiful life as a great dad and phenomenal sibling. I can literally count on him for anything.

The modest home of my childhood was small and simple, with one outdoor bathroom that was located some seventy-five feet from the house. It was a home of sweet tea, corn bread, pinto beans, and the best damn potato soup a cold-and-flu-riddled kid could ever ask for. My mom and dad worked their tails off to start and build a strong family unit. My parents were determined to raise two boys who would become strong men and loving fathers who could and would make a difference in the world.

Life on the farm was simple and good. We didn't have a lot of material stuff. Instead, most of my childhood was spent outside, riding my tricycle and pretending to be a Major League Baseball pitcher in training, substituting apples for the ball and a propped-up board for a catcher behind home plate. With my parents working in the tobacco field, I spent a lot of time with my grandmother Ruby, one of God's greatest blessings in life. She and I would sit on her front porch and eat ice cream until we had "brain freeze," a painful but sure sign that we were having a great time. Life was good. My grandma could remember and recite layers and layers of family genealogy for nearly everyone in the county. Her moral compass filled with words like "pretty is as pretty does" still encourages me today. As I delivered her eulogy on a hot August day in 1995, I felt completely inadequate in expressing my love, admiration, and appreciation for her. I hope she's looking down from heaven with a smile as I write this book.

My parents began to teach me—at the ripe old age of five—what an old-fashioned work ethic was all about. Getting up at four thirty every morning and finishing breakfast a half hour later, we would hurry off to the tobacco field. I never had a curfew—getting up well before dawn naturally dictated going to bed early the night before.

One of my first jobs on the farm was "picking up bones," the stem part of the tobacco plant that was broken off during the harvesting process. I worked at the barn, where workers—usually women—loaded the "picked" tobacco onto a conveyor belt. There, a "stringer" mechanism bound the leaves to a stick that was then used to hang them for drying. An arm on the stringer was supposed to drop down and chop the string once the leaves were bound. But the arm was broken, so my job was to stand there and push down on the arm every fifteen seconds or so to ensure that it chopped the string at the appropriate point in the process. Needless to say, it was tedious to stand there all day pushing down on that metal arm.

One day, Uncle Joe drove up in his truck, saw me standing there, and decided he had a better plan for me to do the job. Everyone, including my dad, loved Uncle Joe—who was actually my great-uncle—but he could be a real smart-ass and a big practical joker. Uncle Joe's plan? Pull up a bucket and take a seat while I kept a watch on that metal arm. It was great! I was so glad to be able to sit down for once.

But my dad was having none of that. He was making the rounds, checking on all the workers between the field and the barn, when he pulled up in his truck, got out of the cab, took his cigar out of his mouth, and hollered at my uncle, "What the hell are you doing?"

"I'm just making it easier for the boy," Uncle Joe told my dad.

My dad had a few other choice words, then basically ran my uncle away from the barn and tossed the bucket aside. I was back on my feet for the duration. Looking back, I'm sure my uncle Joe knew the bucket wouldn't go over well; it was just another way for him to rib my dad.

Working the stringer was the only job I could do at that young age, but over time, my role grew to include more responsibility. By age seven, I was driving tractors and doing more heavy-duty work around the farm. Some of that included hoeing the rows of tobacco, chopping out the weeds between each stalk. By age ten, I had grown into the role of harvesting or "pulling" the tobacco. I went stalk to stalk and pulled three or four leaves at a time, using one hand to break the leaves off and then tuck them under my other arm. When I couldn't hold any more leaves, I'd drop my load off at the nearest trailer, then go back to the row and keep working until the entire row was worked. At the end of that row, I'd turn around and head back down the next row. I did that row after row—it was backbreaking.

Since I wasn't a smoker, promptly at three o'clock in the afternoon every day, I would spend five minutes vomiting violently, purging my body of the nicotine that came from the tobacco leaf touching my skin. The leaves had a residue, a gum, that absorbed into my skin, and its toxic effects struck me daily like clockwork. It was hell, but afterward, I felt great.

The work was hot and hard, and the days were long. Some nights, after fourteen hours in the field, I had to decide whether to eat supper or take a shower since I didn't have the energy to do both.

Harvest began in July and went through September, sometimes into October. During the first three months of harvest, it was hot as Hades—ninety-two to ninety-five degrees Fahrenheit with the same level of humidity. That's the norm in the Piedmont region of North Carolina. It was so hot that some days we started even earlier, arriving at the fields when it was still pitch black. My dad was worried about the workers getting heatstroke, so we'd get to the field in time to be there "when you can see your hand in front of you," as my dad would say. That was the work whistle, so to speak, that signified it was time to begin. We were so early that sometimes we sat there fifteen or twenty minutes waiting on the "hand test."

On the days we started work at five o'clock in the morning, my dad would show up at eight thirty with a special treat—ice-cold RC Colas and MoonPies. On really special days, sausage biscuits made their way to break time. At age ten or twelve, seeing my dad's truck pull up and knowing what was coming made me one happy camper. That was a bright spot in the day.

After break, we would work until noon, take thirty or forty-five minutes for lunch, then head back to the field. Many days, we worked until nightfall, but when it was one-hundred-plus degrees, there were other tasks besides harvesting.

Sometimes that included moving scalding-hot sixteen-foot-long aluminum pipes from one field to another. The pipes were used to irrigate the fields, sometimes drawing water from a pond nearly a quarter mile away. Inevitably, about eight out of ten times, after spending three hours connecting the pipes, something would be wrong with the system—the pipes would leak, or a washer in a pipe would break down, or the pump down at the pond wouldn't start. To this day, every farmer in North Carolina will tell you that watering is the hardest, most frustrating part of the business. It is absolutely hellish. First you have to wade out into a freshly irrigated field, shin deep in sandy mud, unhook a submerged pipe, then load the pipe onto your shoulder, and carry it to a trailer to move it to the next field. There you are, balancing a couple of those scorching-hot pipes on your shoulder, and often they are filled with sand from the field. Between the heat and the sand, they could rub a bare shoulder raw. It wasn't as tough on some of the workers who wore shirts. But it was so hot that for me, the fewer clothes, the better.

There were few dull moments in the field. Since the fields were always near a water source for irrigation, which was often a pond, it wasn't uncommon to find a snake wrapped around the base of a stalk. When harvest starts, the tobacco is typically about chest high. Harvesting involves pulling about four leaves off each plant, starting at the bottom and working to the top. There are about four harvests to clean an entire field. At the start of harvest, you might be working at the base of a plant, but even though the leaves overhead provided a canopy, in 95-degree weather with 95 percent humidity, it felt like 120 degrees at the bottom of a tobacco plant. It was a good day when we did the "last pulling," because that meant pulling the four leaves at the top versus the bottom. When working at the base of the plant, I'd be bent over, going stalk to stalk pulling leaves—and then be surprised by a black snake—or worse, a moccasin—wrapped around the base of a stalk. One summer, we killed twenty-eight snakes.

To get a little relief from the long summer days, I sometimes played practical jokes on—and with—the other farmworkers and my cousin, Jay. From painting my brother's face to give the appearance of chicken pox to putting smoke bombs in Pauline's oven, there was an endless supply of practical jokes. Pauline and her husband, Charlie, were tenants who lived and worked on my father's farm. Back then, they had a bunch of kids at home, and she cooked dinner for her family every night. Before she started dinner one evening, we distracted her to put the bombs in the oven, and when she turned it on, they filled the house with smoke—it looked like the place was on fire. We thought it was hilarious.

On one unfunny occasion, when Jay and I were age seven, we escaped for a day over to Mrs. Vernon's house. She was a neighbor lady who made the best sugar cookies in the world. She let us hang out on her porch swing eating cookies and drinking lemonade. But my mom and Jay's dad, Uncle Jack, couldn't find us and were worried sick. When they finally did find out where we were, they issued a warning that I can still hear today: "You'd better get home before we do." Jay and I ran so fast I swear there was smoke coming off the tires of my little red wagon. But in that race to beat our parents home, we came in second—each of us was promptly greeted with a hickory switch. After that, we didn't "escape" anymore.

Working on the farm was tough, but I appreciated that I was learning the value of a strong work ethic

The vacations we took to places like White Lake, Myrtle Beach, and the mountains were very generous gifts from my parents, who were working eighteen hours a day to build a farming business from ground zero. More often, though, on the last day of school each summer, as my friends headed to the beach to celebrate the break, I would be waving to them from the back plow of the tractor as I worked the field. My job was to stand on the plow so it would go farther into the ground to help soil preparation.

Working on the farm was tough, but I appreciated that I was learning the value of a strong work ethic from my parents—that work ethic would serve me well in life and afford me the luxury one day to literally travel the world.

In fact, here are some of the classic phrases I learned from my dad:

- "You don't work, you don't eat."

- "If you haven't finished your food by now, you don't want it—let's go."

- "I do the thinking; you do the doing."

- "Always do what you say."

- "I've never had a lot of respect for a man that didn't work for himself."

- "You don't need a good memory if you tell the truth."

I have been blessed and have tasted more business success than I ever thought imaginable, due in large part to the sacrifices and real-life lessons from my parents. As I've heard Dave Ramsey say many times over the years, "I'm better off than I deserve."

THE SCHOOL YEARS

My parents' story really was rags to riches, and after their years of hard work, they retired in their early sixties with substantial wealth. Needless to say, entitlement was not an overused word in our family vocabulary. But when it came time for my brother and me to attend school, my parents wanted us to have the best. They made incredible sacrifices to send me to a private school, Piedmont Academy, where I entered first grade at age six.

Back then, school did not start until after Labor Day, since most of the kids attending were from families of farmers. That later start date than what we have today allowed us kids to continue working in the fields through harvest. We'd come home from school and go right to the field until harvest was over. We also did that in April and May, when the weather cooperated, to begin preparing the fields.

The school was filled with teachers who cared about their students, like Mr. Hufflin and Ms. Hodges, along with like-minded parents who worked hard and volunteered so that their children could have a better life.

I was a pretty good student, although slightly more focused on the nonacademic side of my schooling and devious practical jokes. My *first* time in trouble came in the first grade, when I kissed a girl on the playground. A summary of all the other troubles I got into would make *War and Peace* look like a one-page CliffsNotes. For instance, Johnny Hodges and I once spent a solid week fighting, which was only resolved by us being expelled to the school grounds to pick up trash. We laughed and talked the whole time.

One day, at age fifteen, my buddy Allen and I skipped school and caught a ride to UNC with the preacher's wife, who was taking classes there. We went to Carmichael Auditorium, where the Tar Heels played at the time, and we just hung out there all day, shooting hoops and talking to some of the players. One of those players happened to be Phil Ford, one of Carolina's all-time great point guards.

It was an amazing day for someone who had been a Tar Heels fan since birth, and it was made even more special because I got to meet legendary coach Dean Smith. These men embodied *great* Tar Heels basketball tradition. Allen and I had spotted Coach Smith on the way back to his office, and we quickly ran over to say hello and have the privilege of shaking his hand. But the first words out of his mouth were "Why aren't you boys in school?" He then spent the next twenty minutes telling two fifteen-year-old punks about the importance of getting a good education.

Years later, after Coach Smith had retired, my daughter and I attended a Tar Heels game at the Smith Center, affectionately known as the Dean Dome, where the teams have played since the late 1980s. My daughter was around twelve years old, and it was her first UNC game. We had good seats very close to the court, thanks to my dad and his friend Mr. Koury. When the game was over, we were leaving our seats and looked up at the luxury boxes—and there was Dean

Smith! I pointed him out to my daughter and told her to "hold up a second." I then pulled out a piece of paper and wrote a quick note: "Coach Smith, would you please sign an autograph for my daughter?" I handed the paper to the security guard, who told us to wait where we were. We watched as he went into the box and handed the paper to Dean Smith, who then read it and shook his head no. I thought, *Wow. This is just not who I know this man to be.* He was such a gracious man that I couldn't imagine him turning away a twelve-year-old fan. Since I thought that's what was happening, my daughter and I started walking farther up the steps toward the exit when the security guard came up to us, handed me the note, and said, "I'm sorry, sir. Coach Smith doesn't want to give an autograph. He wants to talk to your daughter."

Dean Smith, one of the most legendary coaches of all time, invited my twelve-year-old daughter into the luxury box at Smith Center and then spent twenty minutes talking with her about basketball, school, and life. At the end, he hugged my daughter and then had someone snap a picture of them together. That's the kind of man he was.

I loved and admired Coach Smith so much that even before meeting him, I had publicly vowed to family and friends that I would attend his funeral one day, if at all possible. Thirty-nine years later, I interrupted a two-week business trip in California to fly to Chapel Hill and attend his funeral with my daughter, along with twelve thousand other people who dearly loved the legend.

Although I loved professional sports, I was an average athlete all through high school. I played on all the teams—no choice in the matter, really. Boys were scarce in the high school. Altogether, there were only eleven kids in my graduating class.

One football game in particular, when we played a much larger high school (actually, they all were much larger), we were decimated by injuries and finished the game with only eight players. Most of our football team was composed of guys who also worked in the fields. Instead of having practice like normal kids at three o'clock in the afternoon, we would have practice at seven o'clock at night so that the boys could leave school, go work in the field, and then come back for football practice. Those were long days, and the training was brutal. The coach had the mentality that we would train like Navy SEALs, and he put us through workouts so hard that the games were actually easier than practice sessions. That made us a bunch of tough-as-nails farm boys out on the playing field, but we had to be because we were always outmatched. To give you a visual, there were only thirteen of us on the team, and we would pull up in a rickety bus when we went to other schools. When other teams would visit our school, they would show up in a couple of Greyhounds, and about forty players would come piling out.

Basketball was my favorite sport, and since its season was opposite of harvest, I was able to spend hours and hours every day playing on my homemade court on the farm. Without the nuisance of a defender, I had one hell of an outside shot and an even better free throw—that allowed me to imagine myself retiring from the NBA. Sometimes, a couple of other farm guys like Earl and Wayne would join me, and we'd play until dark.

That was our entertainment. There were no video arcades back then. We didn't go hang out at the pizza shop. We played sports, or we would spend the time fishing, shooting, or hunting deer, squirrels, rabbits, quail, or other game on the tobacco farm or other area farms.

THE PRODIGAL

Sometimes, I had a little too much fun outside of school. One night, just before a school dance, my friend Al and I had a brilliant idea. I talked one of the workers on the farm, Hezekiah, into buying us a six-pack of beer (disgusting and cheap). Not having any real experience with alcohol at that point, I finished one (barely) and then placed another one in the jacket of my leisure suit (imagine a blond John Travolta from *Saturday Night Fever*). I was planning to sneak the beer into the school dance, but the principal intercepted me at the door and suggested that we take a little stroll to his office. Along the way, he told me I was his favorite student in the school. But for my bad decision, I was given the choice of calling my parents myself—otherwise he would make the call. It was one of the hardest calls I've ever had to make.

When my dad returned the following day from a hunting trip—ending it early to deal with his "hell-raising" son—he warned me to "never do that again" in a tone that told me he meant business. I heard him loud and clear.

Later that summer, my life was altered forever. One warm evening in 1979, I was invited by friends to attend a rather large church in nearby Danville, Virginia. During the service, a guest minister preached a message on the prodigal son from Luke 15. In the passage, a rebellious teenager runs away from home because he had "a better idea on how to run his life." Not an uncommon story, then or now.

What struck me that night had little to do with the boy and everything to do with the dad. In the passage, as the wayward boy returned home, broken and empty, the father ran out to greet him. The father hugged his son and ordered new clothes and even a celebratory feast. As I listened to the story, I saw my own hardworking dad coming up the tobacco farm's long driveway to welcome me home and show me compassion. In spite of all the hard work that I put in on that farm, my dad had always had my best interests at heart, and he had loved me unconditionally.

Even more impactful, I realized that's how God welcomes me to him every day—as an errant and arrogant kid. As the great theologian C. H. Spurgeon once said, "I'm pretty sure that if God hadn't pursued me, I would never have pursued him." That night, in his sovereignty, the God of the universe intercepted my trajectory, and I became an everlasting child of Abba's family.

CHAPTER 3

THE ROAD BENDS

On a sweltering summer day in July 1985, I found myself sitting in the cool, air-conditioned office of Bob Jones III, PhD, the chancellor of Bob Jones University (BJU) in Greenville, South Carolina. It was a big, imposing office, mahogany paneled floor to ceiling and furnished with a big mahogany desk. Two security guards were posted outside the office, and inside, there I was, a twenty-two-year-old college student sitting face to face with the chancellor, who had a vehement look on his face and veins popping from his neck.

Clearly angry, he leaned over his desk and, straining to control his voice, said, "Chuck, unless you denounce Jerry Falwell and WLFJ (Christian radio) publicly from the chapel pulpit, you will not be allowed back on campus."

I couldn't believe it. At the time, I was in a leadership role at the school and had just completed my last credits toward my degree. But all that I had learned—and all that I had seen—left me feeling angry, wronged, disillusioned, and dejected. In my six years of being a believer, I just didn't think Jesus treated folks that way.

Shortly after that ultimatum and the completion of my degree, I would leave the campus of BJU. I would not return to my alma mater for sixteen years.

SALVATION AT AGE SIXTEEN

I had chosen BJU because it would allow me to further my beliefs and get an excellent education—at the time, it was the largest Christian university in the United States. And I had bought into those beliefs wholly throughout a good portion of my years at the university.

After my experience at the church in Danville, Virginia, at age sixteen, I had become part of the Christian fundamentalist movement. It was a very conservative sect of Christianity and a different type of religiousness from what I had been raised with by my parents.

I became very involved in the university and church and in all kinds of activities that were centered around the fundamentalist Christian faith. I went to church every Sunday morning, Sunday night, and Wednesday night. I went to revivals. I participated in youth groups. I just immersed myself in the faith.

Already at that age, I had the gift of public speaking. In recognition of that, I was actually invited to speak on some Wednesday nights at the church. I spoke in front of in-person audiences of thousands, but also to a much larger audience when the services were televised.

Several people played big roles in my connection with the church, including Tim and Karen Daniel, who were also the biggest influencers in my going to BJU; Mr. Todd, a kind and gentle soul with a big heart who was over the youth department; Mr. Dalton, a very funny and smart, well-balanced Christian who was a local police detective; and the pastor, whom everybody called Preacher Bradley. He had started the church forty-five years earlier and had served as its only pastor. Even at age eighty-eight, he was still preaching every service in his suit and tie and polished shoes. That—and a hat—was what he always wore, unless he was working on the church building, which he often did. Anything that needed to be done at the church, he was on it. I can still see him in my mind's eye, fixing a broken water pipe or repairing the roof. He did work that some twenty-eight-year-olds could not do. I would often work alongside him doing yard work or helping out with repairs at the church. He never asked me to do anything without also doing the work himself.

Preacher Bradley was a very stern, somewhat gruff man, but he was a great person and a pioneer in the faith—certainly for me. He was really my original mentor in the Christian faith, and I spent a lot of time with him just before he retired. He had been in ministry for some seventy years by then, and out of concern for his health, I asked him one day, "Preacher Bradley, when are you going to retire?"

He replied, "Chuck, I will never retire. I'm only going to retread." I loved the man dearly and cherished every moment I had with him.

OFF THE FARM

Outside the church, I was also influenced by a large Christian radio station, WWMO, 102.5 FM. It became my source of encouragement, and I listened to it every day.

One day, I heard an announcement over the radio that the station needed volunteers for its annual telethon, so I went and helped out by answering phones. I fell in love with the people there, and a couple of weeks later, I approached David Salyers, the general manager, about an internship. He agreed to give me a shot and, a few days later, came to me with a small piece of paper with the weather forecast written on it. "Chuck, you're going to be our weatherman today," he said.

"Holy cow," I said. "What does that mean?"

"You're going to read the weather forecast on the air, live," he answered.

I thought I would surely die on air. I was so nervous; I wasn't even sure I'd be able to read what was written. Sure enough, I stumbled through the reading. But when I was done, Mr. Salyers said, "Great job. I'm going to get you to do that again." After that, I started reading the weather on air almost daily.

Then one day, Mr. Salyers asked me if I'd like to have my own block of time on the radio. The station was going to have an opening from midnight to six o'clock in the morning, and he was asking me to be the announcer (DJ) during that time. I gladly took the paying job, but I would have done it for free—that's how much I loved it. I had control over the songs that were played and the announcements that were made.

I took the job even though I already had a job working in the cotton mill in Danville, Virginia—a shift that started at eight o'clock in the morning. So after I worked all night at the radio station, I would lie down in the station's soundproof production room and sleep for an hour; then I would drive to the cotton mill, where I worked until four o'clock in the afternoon. After work at the mill, I'd grab something to eat, lie down and sleep for a few hours, and then be back at the radio station at midnight.

It was a grueling schedule, but I loved getting the experience at the radio. I even created my own program called *Old-Fashioned Musical Melodies*. At one point, I hired a professional voice-over narrator who created an introduction to the program that went, "Hello! Welcome to *Old-Fashioned Musical Melodies* with Chuck Crumpton." I started the show with that introduction; then I'd play songs and give some stories behind the songs. As I got more comfortable with being on the air, I developed my own radio personality—very down home, folksy, and warm.

Since it was a powerful one-hundred-thousand-watt radio station, one of the few in the country at that time, it had a huge geographical coverage, reaching from Maine to Miami. One morning, at around two o'clock, I mentioned something on the air about being hungry. Almost immediately, the phone began ringing off the hook with people wanting to bring me chicken, biscuits, pie—a late-night picnic. Another time, I was so exhausted from working two jobs that I fell asleep on the air. I had put on a long-play album and didn't wake up until someone called and said, "Chuck, you've got dead air"—which is death for a radio personality. That only happened once. Still, I loved that job so much that even when there was a foot of snow on Christmas Day—which is a massive amount of snow in North Carolina—I drove the thirty miles to the station to make sure I did my show. My mom was very kind and understanding as I left the family Christmas meal to make the trek over. She was always quick to support me in my desires and endeavors.

I loved that station so much that I would later approach its owner, George Beasley, to try to buy it. At the time, he wanted $7.5 million for it—which would be a bargain today—but even though I had a businessman and an attorney join me in the attempted acquisition, we were too far apart in negotiations with Mr. Beasley to put a deal together.

At age sixteen, I also thought I would seriously consider a baseball career, but it basically began and ended on the same day. I had been working on my skills as a pitcher and managed to make it to being named the starting pitcher on game one of the season. But I was so excited to be out on the mound that my first pitch went about twenty-five feet straight up. Horribly embarrassed, I looked over at the coach, who just acknowledged my rookie mistake and mouthed, "Calm down." I managed to stay in the game—long enough to walk the next four batters. The coach took me out of the game as pitcher. My confidence shaken, I struck out every time at bat. I was humiliated, and it surely didn't help me with my new girlfriend.

To top it off, even though I had an awesome Ford Thunderbird that my dad had given me for my sixteenth birthday, and I drove my girlfriend to the game to watch me play, she dropped me after that— she was too embarrassed to be seen with me, a guy who apparently didn't have much of a future in baseball.

THE COLLEGE YEARS

Eventually, I had to leave both of my jobs to attend college. It was especially painful to give up the radio job, but I was destined to go to college, and my parents would have killed me if I had pursued any other course.

I had wanted to go to UNC because I was a die-hard Tar Heels fan, and it was actually closer to my parents' home, where I still lived. As we say in the South, "I was not raised a Tar Heel; I was jerked up as a Tar Heel." But in all honesty, had I gone to UNC, I probably would have been dead or in jail because I had a propensity to party and have fun. I still feel like something of a frat boy today, but back then, at age eighteen, I certainly wouldn't have made it through life at UNC, which may have the nation's largest per capita beer drinking for a small town.

Instead, I chose BJU. The university started in 1927 and was set on a beautiful three-hundred-plus-acre campus. Back then, it enrolled some seven thousand students, all of whom were required to attend chapel every morning at eleven o'clock.

We had thirty-six bells a day that started at 6:55 a.m. and ended at 11:00 p.m. Every bell meant something different. There was one bell to get out of bed in the morning, another bell to put your feet on the floor, another bell to go to class, another bell to go to lunch, another bell to go to chapel. Thirty-six bells a day that required some course of action. There were no TVs for the student body, and there was only one approved radio station that you could listen to.

The cafeteria fed 2,500 people at one time, in twenty minutes. We marched in, ate, and then marched out.

The boys' and the girls' dorms were on opposite sides of campus, and the girls' dorms were very close to the cafeteria—maybe one hundred yards away and heavily monitored. At night, after the evening meal, if you had a girlfriend, you could walk her back to her dorm. That walk came to be called "the longest walk in college history" because it would take guys an hour to walk their girls back to their dorms.

Of course, there was no touching. In fact, there was a six-inch policy—you could never be closer than six inches to your boyfriend or girlfriend. There was a dating parlor where couples could get together, but again, no touching in any way. Monitors would carefully watch to make sure no one was touching. You couldn't even share a magazine because they were afraid that you might hold hands under it.

It was also a school that battled with racial issues and sexual abuse allegations. No African Americans were admitted from the school's inception in 1927 until 1971. As a result of that policy, the school lost its tax-exempt status in 1983 in a Supreme Court case, Bob Jones University v. United States. The ban on interracial dating was finally lifted in 2000, when then governor George W. Bush visited the school during his run for president, and the same Bob Jones III whom I mentioned at the beginning of this chapter appeared on *Larry King Live*. In my opinion, the national media uproar that ensued led to the school lifting its ban on interracial dating for the first time in its history.

The school's board also had a very controversial and divisive figure, Ian Paisley. He had been a member of British Parliament and, while living in Northern Ireland, had had his house and cars bombed. At one point, Paisley's visa was even revoked because he was such a volatile figure.

Paisley was a frequent speaker at the university. In an auditorium that held seven thousand people, his voice was so loud and booming that they would turn off the microphones—because he didn't need them.

I started classes in September 1981, and my first week on campus, for the first time in my life, I had a roommate. I actually had three roommates—four guys in a small dorm room that had four bunk beds, no bath. The bath was always down the hall.

My first day of class, I was already running late, and I asked my senior roommate, Eric, to stop by my class on the way to his and "let the professor know I'm running a little bit late."

He just looked at me with a smart-ass grin, rubbed his hands together, and said, "This is going to be a fun year." Eric more or less terrorized me the whole first year. He was always reading John Molloy's *Dress for Success*, which was his manual for getting dressed every day. He'd see me getting dressed and make comments like "You're seriously going to wear that out in public?" Still basically "just off the farm," I really struggled to know how to dress appropriately.

It didn't take me long to realize why Eric had made his first-day comment. When I got to class, the professor gave me a "What the hell do you think you're doing arriving late to my class?" look that reminded of the TV character Sergeant Carter and his reaction to the always-late Gomer Pyle.

In spite of getting off on the wrong foot, I had a good freshman year and actually became very popular. I made student treasurer with more votes than any freshman for any major office in the history of the school. But before I was sworn in, I lost my chair because I had too many demerits.

BJU was disciplined on a demerit system. If you didn't clean your room, you'd get five demerits. Late to class, fifteen demerits. Getting caught dating off campus was fifty demerits. Seventy-five demerits, and you became what was known as PC, or permanently campused. At that point, you were not allowed to go off campus, hold any office at the school, or date anyone. One hundred and fifty demerits, and you were expelled, or what was known as "shipped."

After I was elected treasurer, but before I was sworn in, I was stripped of my place on the student council because I was PC with seventy-six demerits. I had gone to a church function in Greenville with my mom, and I sat beside a young lady who went to the same church. She wasn't a girlfriend or even a date, but she was sitting there on my left. Never mind that my mom was on my right; someone from the school saw me sitting next to that young lady and reported me for dating off campus. Since I already had twenty-six demerits, the fifty I was given for "dating off campus" put me over the limit. To make matters worse, when I was PC, I wasn't allowed to talk to the young lady whom I *was* dating, so that relationship came to an end. I was stripped of all my dignity, my pride, my newly elected power, and my girlfriend.

Fortunately, that was the end of demerits for that semester, and they started over again each semester. Of course, when you were PC, unless you did some really stupid, there weren't really a lot of opportunities to get in a whole lot more trouble.

Still, I recall my first couple of years at BJU as being a good experience. On weekends, we would leave the campus and go to work in local churches in the area.

On one of those trips when I was a sophomore, I was in a Ford Pinto with three other students, and we were driving to Statesville, North Carolina. When we stopped to get gas, one of the guys put diesel fuel in the car. Ironically, Dan was the only PhD student in our group—very smart but not much common sense. We caught him just as he was pulling the nozzle out of the car, so without really knowing what to do, we headed on down the road. We were hoping to run the diesel out of the system, then fill it back up with gas. Instead, the car broke down on Interstate 40, about twenty miles outside of Asheville, North Carolina. It was a cold, brisk Saturday, about four thirty in the afternoon. The sun would be dropping in about an hour, and there we were, in a remote area of the interstate outside Asheville.

I decided to hike to the nearest gas station and actually caught a ride with a highway patrolman. He dropped me off at the BP gas station about ten miles down the road, just before closing time at five o'clock. The owner's name was Jerry, a man who turned out to be an angel of God. There it was, closing time on a Saturday, and Jerry got out his wrecker and drove me back to where the others were waiting in the car. He hooked up the car, drove it and us to the gas station, and then spent two hours flushing out the fuel lines. We were broke college kids with thirteen dollars between us, so we had no idea how we were going to pay him for the work. Nevertheless, when he finished, I asked him, "Jerry, how much do we owe you?"

He just said, "Boys, give me ten dollars, and just get on the road." After towing us for ten miles and then working two hours on the car, he charged us ten dollars.

I will never forget that act of kindness as long as I live. Years later I drove to Asheville just to say thanks to Jerry and to let him know the little band of gypsies he had rescued turned out pretty well.

Another act of unforgettable kindness came during my junior year, when I spent every other weekend working for a very remote, tiny church in Sylva, North Carolina. They tapped me to be their interim choir director and to work with the youth there, even though I really couldn't read music. Over the weekend, I would stay with Bobby and Ethel McMahon. I slept in their basement, and every Sunday morning, Ethel would make "cat head" biscuits the size of a saucer along with homemade gravy. I woke up every Sunday morning to the smell of that gravy and southern gospel music playing.

After lunch, we would go to Grover McMahon's house, and his wife, Evelyn, always had a massive mountain meal of four meats and seven vegetables prepared. There was so much food that one time I told Grover, "Grover, I can't eat any more; I'm busting out of my clothes."

He looked at me and said, "Chuck, that's why you buy bigger clothes—so you can eat more." It was a beautiful part of the country, and I got to be there with absolutely beautiful people who led such simple lives. Their sole entertainment every week was going to church and playing bluegrass music on Saturday night.

Those off-campus adventures were some of the fondest memories I have of college, and I carry them with me to this day.

HYPOCRISY AND BULLSHIT

Over time, I became more entrenched in the university—and I became more steeped in the legalism of fundamentalist Christianity.

For example, since I was taught by the school that alcohol was wrong, I would not stop at a gas station that sold beer. One time, I even ran out of gas because I couldn't find a station that didn't sell beer. At one point during those years, I was responsible for booking an event with a very well-known singing group from a large church in the area. Being young and arrogant, I called up the pastor and said, "Pastor, I just have one question. Does the hair of the men touch their ears?"

I held everyone and everything to an overwhelmingly high standard, a standard that was nowhere close to biblical standards. Basically, I became a real asshole

He was silent for a moment (stunned into silence, I'm sure), then answered, "Well, son, I don't know. There are fifty people in this group. I don't keep up with that."

I replied, "I'm sorry, sir. I can't allow them to sing if their hair touches their ears."

Instead of trying to enhance my relationship with God, I developed a real checklist mentality based on a bunch of dos and don'ts. I thought that if I did all the right things and didn't do the wrong things that I would be accepted by God more. Later, I would realize that was a bogus mindset. But before I reached that point, I became a bully to my family and friends. I held everyone and everything to an overwhelmingly high standard, a standard that was nowhere close to biblical standards. Basically, I became a real asshole.

During college, I did not go to movies, did not smoke, did not do drugs. I was probably one of the few students ever in the history of college who never drank a sip of alcohol during those years. (I've made up for it since.) I used to have massive guilt episodes after doing something that normal college-age kids do. God never intended that for his children.

Over time, something did not sit right with me, and I began to see a lot of hypocrisy and bullshit.

At the end of my junior year, I was selected for the position of resident assistant (monitor), a very prestigious job that came with a lot of responsibilities. I was one of twenty-six monitors on a campus of seven thousand students. I was responsible for seventy young men on my hall, and I had to enforce all the rules and standards of the university. I had to check to make sure their rooms were clean and that they were on time for chapel. I had to be up at 6:55 a.m. to make sure my guys were up, and I had to make the rounds every night at 11:00 p.m. to ensure they were all in bed. It was really almost a full-time job, which fortunately did come with some pay.

My role as RA gave me a lot of access to what was going on behind the scenes. The other RAs and I met regularly with the senior leadership of the university, including Dr. Jones. In addition to him, I had a lot of access to the president and the deans, so I saw a lot of things behind the scenes that really began to bother me.

For instance, every night, after we had made sure everyone was in their beds, the RAs gathered for what was called a "monitors' meeting." In those meetings, we were allowed to eat popcorn and watch TV shows like *Gunsmoke* and *Twilight Zone*—remember, TVs weren't available to anyone else on campus. Even worse, after the shows were over, talk would begin about students who were "not Bob Jones material." One night, the target was two brothers from the

Midwest—it was even determined that their lockers, rooms, and cars would be searched to find some kind of evidence to get them thrown out of school.

I began to see more and more of that "gestapo mentality," and it didn't resonate with me. I started to see how my own "checklist mentality" wasn't how I wanted to conduct my life. It wasn't how I wanted to lead.

I was so conflicted in my own spirit that I began to question the integrity and morality of the school.

Then, at one point, one of the guys on my hall came to me. "Chuck, I need to share something with you," he said. Mike C., as I'll call him, sat on the edge of my bed and said, "I keep a journal of my life every day, and I need to share some very painful things out of it."

"Sure, Mike; talk to me," I told him.

"Chuck," he said, pausing and taking a deep breath. "I am a homosexual. I am gay." Then he handed me his journal and said, "I want you to read what my life looks like every day." In it, he had chronicled the incredible amount of pain and guilt he had felt over seeing other guys in the shower, masturbation, and being in conflict with his family about his sexuality. He and I both knew that if anybody in the school found out about his sexuality, he would immediately be shipped. But he had a high-profile position at the school, and the only way he would be able to afford college was to keep his job and stay there at the school.

As he sat there and poured his heart out to me, he cried like a baby. I could just see the enormous amount of pain that he was going through every single day of his life as he tried to reconcile his faith and his sexuality.

It was my first experience in dealing with someone who was gay, and I sat there thinking, "I'm not equipped to help him. All I can do is to love this guy and care for him and be his friend." I didn't know what to do other than put my arm around him and say, "Mike, this will stay between you and me."

I truly felt his pain, but afterward, I began to feel real anger. Here was a man who was sincere in his faith, but he was prohibited from going to anybody in an official capacity to say, "This is who I am; this is my life."

That episode really stirred up in me a level of anger because of the hatred and the intolerance that I experienced at the school and the fundamentalist paradigm.

Every day, I found myself struggling with that anger, and it opened my eyes even more. Everywhere I looked, I began to see hypocrisy. Looking back, I know that my behaviors were very immature—I just couldn't seem to communicate what needed to be said in a proper way.

My frustration and anger built to the point that I should have resigned from my role as RA. Instead, I stayed in my position and became arrogant—and more vocal. I had decided I needed to make a change in the way things were. I felt like I could make a difference in the lives of these seventy guys whom I was responsible for by being real, by being transparent, and by loving them where they were in life. These were eighteen-, nineteen-, twenty-year-old men who had differences of opinion with their faith, with their sexuality, with whatever. And I felt like I could be a friend; I could make a difference.

But all of that was in conflict with the views of BJU at the time.

Finally, one night, somebody overheard the dorm supervisor saying, "We're going to relieve Chuck of his duties." Word spread quickly, and there was literally a revolt in the dorm. All the guys came out into the halls and started chanting my name: "Chuck, Chuck, Chuck."

I was called into the dorm supervisor's office that night, where I was told I had put the university in a position of no return. They decided to keep me in my role, but I would basically be a lame duck.

That was early April 1985, and I graduated two months later. That's when I was called into Dr. Jones's office, where he lowered the boom.

THERE IS HOPE

After I left BJU, like a lot of students of fundamentalism, I went through a period where I swung from one extreme to the other in my walk and Christian practices. I've seen literally hundreds of kids be affected by the negative parts of fundamentalism, where they are taught such conservative thoughts that when they come out from under the rule of the administration or under their parents' thumbs, they go crazy. They go nuts. I definitely got

It's not about rules, but it's about a relationship

into alcohol and some other crazy stuff, but not drugs or sexual immorality or anything to the extent that I saw in so many others. But I definitely swung the other way from fundamentalism. And that's not a balance. That's not a healthy position to be in.

Certainly, when I came out of BJU, my Christianity and relationship with God was affected. I was unbalanced. I was unstable. I felt abandoned. It made me intensify my scrutiny of every religious organization. I looked at everything with a jaded paradigm. I thank God that I came to realize that it's not about rules, but it's about a relationship. I think a lot of people need to hear that. Reflecting back, now more than thirty years since my graduation from Bob Jones, I realize a couple of things. First, I was naive, arrogant, and lacking in how I characterized BJU in its approach and conduct. I don't think I was wrong in my perceptions of the school, but I could have been so much wiser and humbler in some of my reactions to the school and how it lived out its ideology. Life has taught me some hard lessons since then. Secondly, I am very grateful for the education I received there. I learned a lot about academics and life, and I'm incredibly grateful for my parents, who made the sacrifices to send me to college.

Since then, I have found that some people and some organizations are just doing it right. They're not betraying the confidence of the people who hold them dear and near. They have full integrity.

There is hope for people coming out of religious handcuffs into a true, healthy, balanced, relationship with God. In fact, reflecting back, I realize that there are five truths to remember as you seek your own faith balance.

1. Don't allow any organization to rob you of true joy.

2. Be careful what you devote your time to, because time is so precious.

3. People will let you down.

4. Be quick to forgive and to ask for forgiveness.

5. Don't allow man-made rules to put you in a box.

During my own pendulum swing, two things helped me get back to where I should be with God. One was a book, *Abba's Child: The Cry of the Heart of Intimate Belonging*, by Brennan Manning, in which he talks about his life as a Catholic priest and becoming an alcoholic. One day, in his extreme struggle with life and his addiction, he spent some time alone in the mountains and realized for the first time in his life that he was a child of God; he was Abba's child. He realized that he could call out to Abba, to his Father. It is the most wonderful thing in the world to get to that point, after being so paralyzed by religion, that you recognize there is a God who just loves you for who you are, for where you are in life.

The other thing that helped me was a story told to me by one of my dearest friends in the faith, a pastor by the name of Eddie West. At one point, Pastor West had resigned from his role with the church. One day after that, he went into his bank, and the teller looked at him and asked, "Are you Pastor West?"

When he looked up at the teller, he saw a dazzled look on that person's face. "Yes," he replied. "Yes, I am Pastor West." After that encounter, Eddie went home, where, for the first time in his life, he "felt the sunshine of God's love."

If you are a recovering fundamentalist or someone struggling with your beliefs as I did, then I hope you will see by my experience that there is hope. That somewhere in that pendulum swing, you will also experience the sunshine of God's love.

CHAPTER 4

ALL DRESSED UP

Oh, by the way, what kind of beer do you like?

It was 1985, and I was fresh out of college, looking for my first real job. The question was asked by Leighton Cubbage, head of field sales for a company called Tel/Man, a telecommunications company based in Greenville, South Carolina. It came while on a tour of the corporate offices after six very in-depth interviews where I'd been asked a lot of hardcore questions to try to determine what kind of salesperson I might be.

He asked me that question during the seventh and final interview as he walked me around the company's two-story building to show me where all the teams were located: operations, sales, customer support, accounting. The last stop on the tour was the company's fitness facilities—after showing me around the room, he opened the back door to let me out to the parking lot, and that's when he asked me about my drink of choice.

The interviews were so extensive and in depth because Leighton (or Cub, as I came to call him) wanted to make sure that I, a graduate of Bob Jones University, could fit the company culture. I was twenty-two and a recent grad, and I would be working with a lot of other twenty-two-to-twenty-five-year-old recent college grads, most from state universities. Like the others on the team, I was a typical young man who played hard and was ready to work hard. But because of the school I had attended, Cub wanted to be certain I could handle the culture of the company. As I mentioned in the last chapter, I didn't drink beer at all during college—before I became disillusioned, I had grown to staunchly believe that any alcohol was wrong.

I ultimately did get hired on in what was my first real job.

In fact, Cub would become one of my very early business mentors, someone who would help me learn the ropes but who would also go on to parlay his entrepreneurialism into enormous success.

Cub graduated from Clemson University in 1977 and had been a football player during his college years. In 1993, he earned an advanced management degree from UNC, and two years later, he was named South Carolina Entrepreneur of the Year.

While his question to me about my favorite brew was memorable, there are other key phrases that Cub shared that have served me well over the years. One that I have adopted as my personal credo is "Work on yourself in every category. Laugh, get around people that you want to be around, and attack life." He really had an unbelievable impact on me. Much of my management experience and business success I owe to my dad and to Cub.

When I called him up to tell him about this book and that I intended to put him in it, we had a very emotional reunion after seven years. It was late on a Wednesday, and Cub told me that he'd had a rough business day that day—one that cost him a lot of money. But he wasn't telling me as a way of dumping his woes on me; he explained that even though he had lost that significant deal, "this phone call meant more to me than that deal."

After I had accepted the offer to work at Tel/Man, but before my first day, I told Cub I would stop in at the Greensboro office to meet some of the people there. But when I arrived, I found out that it was more than a visit—Cub had set up another interview for me to meet with my immediate sales manager, David Hudson. I found out about the interview when David greeted me at the door and said, "We'd like to start the interview in a few minutes." I was in casual clothes and completely taken by surprise. But I didn't let it phase me. After David and other members of the team gathered in David's office, they asked me to leave the room and then come back in as if I was a candidate just interviewing for the first time. I had to role-play getting through the gatekeeper, asking for a meeting, and going through all the standard protocol of a first interview. I came to find out that this was Cub's way of making sure that I was always prepared for battle, that I always brought my A game.

After I was hired, I found out from Judy Slaughter, who oversaw training, that Tel/Man had a very defined paradigm when hiring. Yes, they wanted recent college graduates, typically young people ages twenty-two to twenty-five. But they wanted people with a lot of energy who were very professional, very polished. People with very strong work ethics and very strong value systems. People who were very connected to their families.

As a result of that paradigm, the company had very low attrition—probably around 75 percent less than most companies hiring people straight out of college. Since I saw that paradigm work so well at Tel/Man, I have adopted it as I have built and grown my own businesses over the years.

Although my years at Tel/Man would ultimately shape me into a business executive, I started out pretty low on the ladder. My starting salary was heavily weighted toward commissions. I had a $12,000 a year base along with an incredibly high commission structure. If I was good at sales, I could make a lot of money. That first year, I made around $45,000, which was near the top of the company in sales.

I credit David, my first manager, for shaping my early sales career. He was a graduate of the Citadel. We all loved him and affectionately referred to him as "Hud Man" or "Huddler." Even though he was a hard-driving sales manager, he was also very encouraging and very motivating. He always led by example and never asked that we outwork him. He was the first in the office every morning and the last one to leave. Our office hours were officially eight o'clock in the morning to five thirty in the evening, but for Hud Man, the workday went from seven thirty in the morning to six o'clock in the evening. He was very driven and determined, and it made us all want to work that much harder. In fact, sometimes we were there with him early, and we worked our tails off all day and often stayed later. As a result, we had one of the most successful offices in the company.

That's why it was such a surprise when late one Friday afternoon, David came out of his office, slapped each of us on the back, and told us, "You guys just go ahead and leave; get out of here early today." It was 5:27 p.m., but it was a big deal for Hud—a man who was a professional through and through and who was a stickler for details—to let us go get our cold after-work beer.

I had some phenomenal coworkers in that first job, part of a really great team. We were very tight knit, like minded, and similar in our values. We were friends and cared for each other's success. So we had a lot of fun, even though we worked really hard. After work, we'd hang out together, playing poker or basketball. And on snow days, when the office was closed, we would make golf putts (or try) in the office hallway and do tequila shots after bad shots.

Scott Sawyer, Dwayne Drake, and Ted Hassold were three of my associates and friends whom I'll always remember with great fondness. We all came from different backgrounds, but we shared the same value system, work ethic, and commitment to helping each other, which allowed us to have fun and enjoy success together.

Back then, I was "rough around the edges" but had a lot of potential. I was not real subtle in my approach at all with office politics. One day, Ted pulled me aside to share with me some wisdom that I have lived by ever since. "Chuck," he said, "you've got so much ability and so many gifts. But you tend to be a maverick in your approach with people and procedures. As you build your career, don't forget to take the time to bring people along on your journey."

I was twenty-three years old, but I remember that advice like it was yesterday. Ted was only one year older, but I felt like he was many years wiser. He was also very compassionate, and he cared enough to put his arm around me and help me on the people side. It was care and conversation I will never forget.

GOOD LUCK, BUDDY

I'll never forget my first day on the job. I had gone through a very good training program with Judy's group, which taught me all about the technology we were selling and what kind of activity to expect.

That first day, David met me with a "Welcome to the team." He then walked me down the hall to my office, the fourth one on the right, where he opened the door to let me in. When I entered the room, I found the following: a desk, a chair, a phone, and a phone book.

"Chuck," David said, "good to have you on the team. Good luck, buddy."

Then he patted me on the back and left, closing the door on his way out.

There I stood, looking at the desk, chair, phone, and phone book—sort of like a deer caught in the headlights.

"What the hell am I doing?" I said out loud. "I don't know what I'm doing. I don't know who to call."

Still, there was no turning back at that point, so I sat down, opened up the phone book, and started making calls, trying to set up sales meetings. The first few calls were absolutely terrifying. I had never made a sale for this company in my life, so I didn't know what to say other than what I had been taught by Judy and Cub. But I just kept pounding through the phone book, calling companies and ultimately making twenty-three calls that first day. I still have the call sheet from my first day on the job as a reminder of what it takes to be successful. I learned that when you couple a great attitude with high activity, success will be inevitable.

But it took a while to make my first sale. I was making appointments and doing all the right things—improving my approach, getting more comfortable with the process—but I was dying on the vine. I was desperate to be successful. Everyone knows you've got to fake it till you make it, but all that faking it was wearing me down.

It didn't help that after graduation, I wasted the little bit of money that I had saved up on a piece-of-shit truck that always broke down. I lost all my savings on that truck, so to pay rent and buy food, I ended up getting a janitorial job in the evenings. I would work at Tel/Man until around six or six thirty in the evening; then I would take off my suit, put on shorts and a T-shirt, and go to work for the janitorial company from seven o'clock to eleven o'clock at night. Those were long days.

Sometimes, I would actually clean some of the buildings that I'd had meetings in earlier that week in my sales role at Tel/Man. One time, I was cleaning the office of a client I had met with the day before as part of my sales job, when he came back to retrieve something out of his desk. There I was, dumping out his waste can, when I saw him coming. I quickly ducked around a corner so he wouldn't see me there working my second job.

Finally, I made my first sale. I was about halfway through my sales appointment when the customer looked at me and said, "Let's do it." But I kept talking.

"Okay, I'm sold," the customer said. And I kept talking.

Finally, the customer said, "Chuck, please be quiet. You've made the sale. Let's do the paperwork."

"Okay," I answered. I was so nervous when filling out the paperwork that my hands were shaking.

Afterward, I was so excited that I could barely keep from dancing in the parking lot on the way to my car. I actually pulled over in the parking lot next door and did a little dance to celebrate my first deal. In my management years ahead, I would encourage my folks to dance or sing their success. Don't dull the joy of winning.

Since then, I've clung to some words of encouragement that Cub taught me when I was dying for that first sale. He told me, "Blessed is he that packeth the pipe." That was his way of saying, "Keep building your funnel, keep working, keep knocking on the door, and it will pay off."

THE TURKEY PAGE

The dam broke. After that first deal, I never went a week without making a sale. Although there was one time that I came very close to being listed on "the turkey page."

The turkey page was like the walk of shame for an account manager. Tel/Man had a number of offices throughout the Southeast, and every week, the company would issue a sales report that ranked all the salespeople in the region. If you didn't close a deal that week, your name ended up on the turkey page. Nobody wanted to be on the turkey page.

One week, right before a Fourth of July weekend, I was dangerously close to being on the turkey page. When I got back to the office late the Friday just before the holiday weekend, I still hadn't made a sale. Hud Man greeted me with, "How'd you do? How'd you do?"

But all I could tell him was, "I'm really close on one, but I didn't get it."

In typical Hud fashion, he said, "Okay, that's great. Let's go out and knock on some doors." This was at four thirty in the afternoon on a hot, scorching summer day in North Carolina. It was Friday, when everyone was closing up to head out on a three-day weekend.

But off we went, into the sweltering ninety-eight-degree, humid-as-hell afternoon to knock on doors to try to get a sale—and keep me off the turkey list.

Finally, we found an industrial supply company in Greensboro that was still open. We walked in, only to find them starting to turn off the lights, getting ready to leave. We were on a mission as we talked to the front desk, where the receptionist told us, "Jim is the head of this branch. I think he may be here, but he's getting ready to leave."

We begged the lady for a few minutes and were shown back to the office where we found him packing up his briefcase. We didn't let that stop us. We started making our pitch when Jim said, "Boys, this sounds good, but my family is waiting in the car. We're headed to the beach for the weekend. The car is already running, so I've got to get out of here."

Hud and I both got down on one knee and said, "Please, please, give us a chance." Jim just looked at us, shook his head, and told us he couldn't believe we were out late on Friday afternoon, in North Carolina heat and humidity, just before the Fourth of July weekend, trying to get his business. We ultimately got the account, but I've often wondered if it was only because Jim thought we were insane.

> *Just keep knocking on the door; never, ever give up; and sometimes, you have to beg for the business*

That was part of the work ethic that we were taught—that you just keep knocking on the door; never, ever give up; and sometimes, you have to beg for the business. Those were valuable lessons for me.

CARING LEADERS, COLORFUL CHARACTERS

Cub's boss, Bud Stoner, was the executive vice president of the company. Every week, based on sales success, Bud wrote notes to the top salespeople. He would copy the sales sheet and then write an encouraging note on the sheet in red ink. In those notes, he wrote things like: "Chuck, you're doing great. This has been a good week. Keep up the hard work." I saved those notes because it meant so much to me that the top guy in the company took the time out of his schedule to recognize my efforts and my success. I just found that to be incredibly encouraging, and I still have some of those notes. A few positive words can make a huge difference in a person's life.

I also worked with some colorful characters. One was Norm Shapiro, with whom I competed every week for the top spot. Usually, it was either him or me at the top of the list when it came to sales. Norm was a very colorful Jewish man who had moved his family to Charlotte from New York City. He was a former bra salesman in the Empire State Building, and he used to tell an incredible story about leaving the city when he had decided to relocate. *The Charlotte Observer* would later print this story in one of its feature sections of the paper.

He was leaving the city and heading for Charlotte when his car broke down crossing the bridge in Harlem. This was way back before everyone had a cell phone to call for a tow. He got out of his car and started walking to the nearest gas station to get some help (stepping over a couple of dead bodies, he says), but it was the middle of the night, so everything was closed. Unable to find help, he started walking back to his car. He was still some distance away when he noticed that the car's hood was up. As he approached it, he realized there was a guy working under the hood to try to get the car started. Norm got to the car and said, "Hey, what are you doing?"

"What do you mean, what am I doing? I'm stealing this car," said the thief.

"You can't steal this car. This is my car," Norm told him.

"Look," the thief said. "I've got to get a Chevy Caprice tonight, and this is a Chevy Caprice. As soon as I get it running, I'm going to steal it."

The ever-calm Norm just said, "Look, I'll make a deal with you. If you'll get my car started, I will drive you around until you find another car."

Incredibly, Norm talked the guy into fixing his car, and then he dropped him off a couple of blocks away before driving off—in his own car—to begin his new life in Charlotte. That's the kind of sales skill I competed with every week in my first job.

SHOCK VALUE

There are driven people like Norm whom I am absolutely drawn to in life. People who have a natural-born talent, a great sense of humor, or just an overall outlook that I find inspirational.

Then there are people whose paradigms on life may differ from mine, but whose lives I find to be encouraging and incredibly thought-provoking. Being out in the real world after graduation and in a job that had me talking to people from many walks of life every day opened up my mind to the fact that people are different, and sometimes just listening to them can help me find common ground and have a new perspective on them or even a new perspective on the world.

One of those people is Howard Stern, the shock jock from New York who started his radio career making ninety-six dollars a week and now makes $90 million a year and has a net worth of $650 million. Some thirty million people listen to Howard every day.

What I find encouraging about Howard is his level of vulnerability and transparency. He talks openly about his OCD and all the psychotherapy he's going through. I also see in Howard the same work ethic that I had used to build my early career in business. He used that same drive and work ethic to build what has made him, as some call, "the king of all media."

I find it inspiring that he started out thinking that he would be fired by lunch his first day on the job, and instead he has had an incredible career. Although Howard's path and mine have really been extreme opposites, where I see some commonality is in the craving for real relationships, the vulnerability and transparency, and some common values, including honesty, integrity, a belief in working hard, and a love for his children and his wife. It's just a strange paradox that two people can arrive at a success point in their careers based on very different paths but similar values.

You can learn from anyone. You can be inspired by anyone if you just give them an opportunity to touch your life.

It's amazing to me how our lives evolve. Here's Howard Stern, someone I would never have listened to only a few years ago, but the more I listen to his radio show and read his books, the more I become encouraged and realize that the perception that we have of him is perhaps not close to reality. How many other amazing people are out there whom I've shut off because of my preconceived biases?

The point is, you can learn from anyone. You can be inspired by anyone if you just give them an opportunity to touch your life. Everyone has a message, a story to tell. I want to be better at listening to those stories.

A DIFFERENT KIND OF CRAZY

I was in sales at Tel/Man for four years. Two years into the job, I was promoted to city manager in Asheville, North Carolina. Asheville is a beautiful little city on the Blue Ridge Parkway in the mountains of North Carolina. When I went to Asheville, I took over an office of one because everybody else had left the branch.

It had been an office filled with a lot of testosterone. The month before I came to work at the office, one of the guys who had worked there before had had some kind of fling with one of the girls in town, and she went berserk and came to the office and shot a hole through the door. So I had some stuff to overcome when I first became the city representative for the company, including a very bizarre incident that happened with the tenant on the first floor.

The building was the only high-rise in Asheville at the time, and my office was on the fifth floor overlooking beautiful downtown. Every morning on the way in to work, I would stop in at a coffee shop located in the same building, where I would get a cup of coffee and a newspaper. One day, the woman who ran the coffee shop said to me, "Chuck, it's really good to have you in the building. Just to let you know, I run a travel business on the side. If you ever want discount tickets to the Biltmore or discount hotel reservations at the Grove Park Inn, let me know. I can get them for half off." The Biltmore is the unbelievably beautiful former home of the Vanderbilts that is now a major attraction, and Grove Park Inn is a very prestigious resort.

"That would be great," I told the coffee shop travel agent, but I didn't take her up on her offer right away. The next time I was visiting my parents, my aunt and uncle were there, and when I mentioned the offer to them, my aunt was excited about the chance to finally get to stay at the inn. When I returned to Asheville, I gave the coffee shop travel agent the dates my aunt and uncle wanted to stay at the inn. "Great," she said. "I'll make the reservation and pay for it, and then you can just pay me."

"Wonderful," I told her. "This is great; my uncle and aunt will love it!"

A couple of days later, I received an invoice from the coffee shop travel agent for a two-night stay at the Grove Park at half rate. That's when I asked her, "By the way, what is the cancellation policy?"

"It's normally seventy-two hours," she said. "But don't worry. I do so much business with the Grove Park Inn that if you have to cancel, they'll let me do it within twenty-four hours."

Unfortunately, when it came time for my aunt and uncle to take their trip, my aunt's mother became ill, so they had to cancel. My aunt called me on Monday of that week to let me know they weren't going to make it—in plenty of time to cancel the reservation on Friday. As soon as I hung up the phone, I called the coffee shop travel agent to let her know about the cancellation, and she assured me that the reservation would be cancelled with no penalty.

Well, the following week I got another invoice from the coffee shop travel agent listing the full charges for the reservation. When I called her about it, I said, "Hey, I called you last Monday about canceling the reservation." I recalled the details to her of the whole situation.

"Oh yes," she said, "but it violated their cancellation policies."

"But I told you on Monday, and they were not coming until Friday," I said.

"Look, it is what it is," she just said.

After I hung up, I had an uneasy feeling. I called the Grove Park Inn, and I asked about their cancellation policy. Seventy-two hours, the reservationist told me.

"If I'm working with a travel agent, is it the same?" I asked.

"Sometimes it is," the reservationist said. "Who's your agent?"

I told her, and she looked for the reservation under the coffee shop travel agent's name. Nothing. I asked her to look it up under my name. Nothing. Under my aunt's name. Nothing.

I called the coffee shop travel agent back and told her that I had contacted the resort directly. At that point, she went ballistic. She started screaming and cussing at me and said, "Chuck, pay the damn bill, or I'm going to kill you—literally."

I hung up the phone and was sitting there at my desk, shell shocked. I had never had my life threatened before, so I wasn't exactly sure what to do. I decided to check the office door to make sure it was locked—it was, as a rule after the previous shooting—and when I looked out the peephole, I saw the coffee shop travel agent literally clawing at the door, trying to get in.

This woman is psychotic, I realized. Fearing for my life, I called the Asheville police. Maybe it was a slow day for crime in the little mountain town, or maybe because of the previous incident, help came quickly. After I made the call, I looked out the office window and saw that the streets were blocked off—the SWAT team had been called in. I looked out my peephole again and saw them invade the entire fifth floor. After that, I never saw the coffee shop travel agent again. I do love life's wonderful adventures.

NEVER STOP KNOCKING ON THE DOOR

Working for Cub and David at Tel/Man really gave me insights into the philosophy of leadership. Under their guidance, I learned about commitment to each other, the commitment to the mission, teamwork, work ethic, and always doing the right thing.

In what was really my first job out of college, I learned the principle of push/pull: I'm going to push you, you're going to pull me, and we're going to win together. We're going to look after each other. I witnessed the impact that leadership paradigm had on attrition—it was very, very low.

Although I loved that job, the company, and the people I worked with, after five years of working there, I would leave for another opportunity. Cub had left the company a few months earlier to start his own venture. After I had already been recruited and hired by another company, the phone rang—it was Cub. I was living in Charlotte, and he asked me to come down to Greenville for a visit. "I've got something to share with you," he said.

I drove down to Greenville, and we had a nice steak dinner at T-Bones, after which he asked me to follow him over to the office of a new company, CTG, that he had just started. "Great, Cub. I'd love to see it," I told him. It was getting pretty late, around nine thirty, so we drove over in separate cars, and after we arrived at the office, he unlocked the door and flipped on the lights.

Cub is a big man, so I had to look up to see the reaction on his face. I'll never forget the look in his eyes as he said, "Look at this beautiful office." It was a big open office space with two little desks.

"Cub," I said, "there's nothing here. What's going on?"

"Well," he said, "right now, we play football every Friday in here. But one day, this room is going to be full with people."

Then he started telling me about all the plans he had for the space—including where my office would be. "In five years, we're going to have one hundred twenty-five people in this office space. I've already done the planning," he said. I remember thinking that if anyone could build a company from zero to 125 people, it was Leighton Cubbage.

When he told me that he wanted me to be a part of what was going to be something very special, I asked him to tell me more. "Talk to me, Cub," I said. "What does that look like? What does that mean?"

"Chuck, I'm going to give you a salary of $35,000, but I'm going to give you stock options, and you're going to make a lot of money one day," Cub said. His plan included selling the company five years after its start. "It's going to be beautiful," he said.

Unfortunately, I had a baby girl and a stay-at-home wife at the time, plus a mortgage, two car payments, and plenty of other bills. "Cub," I said, "my salary now is $70,000. It takes me $69,000 to live. I can't live on $35,000."

"Oh, Chuck, you've got to make a way, man," Cub replied. "This is going to be great. I'm going to give you stock options, and you're going to be a wealthy man one day."

I loved that man's vision and enthusiasm more than anything, but I had to turn him down. "Cub," I said, "if anybody can do it, it's you, but I can't pay my bills on $35,000 a year. I just can't."

"You go home; you think about it," he said. "I want you on the team."

As I drove back to Charlotte, I thought, *There's just no way I can do this.* Ultimately, that was my answer to Cub. That was 1990. In 1995, Cub sold that company of 120 people for well over a hundred million, and forty-one people in that company became millionaires.

After he sold the business, Cub and I got together for a game of racquetball. There he was, a man who had come from nothing and was now a multimillionaire, stepping out on the court to play racquetball with me. I was enamored, amazed, encouraged, and so proud of his success and what he and his team had built because they were on a mission together. So I couldn't help but ask, "Cub, what is the secret to your success?"

He just looked at me and said, "Chu Chu [his nickname for me], I just kept knocking on the door. I just kept knocking on the door."

That's how I've built my career ever since: I've just kept knocking on the door.

I find British entrepreneur Sir Richard Branson truly inspirational. There are a number of things that everybody knows about him: his net worth of $5.1 billion, he was knighted in 2000 by the queen of England, and he was named one of the top one hundred most influential people in the world by *Time* magazine. Those are things we know about Richard Branson.

What many people don't know about him is that his first job was selling Christmas trees and birds—and he was a miserable failure at that. We know of his tremendous success with the Virgin brand, but a lot of people don't know that failures under that brand include Virgin Cola and Virgin Cars.

So while he is most known for his overwhelming successes, we sometimes forget the failures and pitfalls and times that he has stumped his toe. "I suppose the secret to bouncing back is not only to be unafraid of failures, but to use them as motivational and learning tools," he has said.[1] Through it all, even Branson knew that the secret to success is to *never stop knocking on the door.*

---

1   Richard Branson, *Like a Virgin: Secrets They Won't Teach You at Business School* (New York: Penguin Group, 2012), 62.

CHAPTER 5

MY WORLD CHANGED— IN AN INSTANT

My world was rocked and changed forever on July 18, 1989— for the better. "It's a beautiful, healthy girl," proclaimed the OB-GYN. Like a tornado, Katie Elizabeth Crumpton, my beautiful, gifted, charming, amazingly giving daughter came screaming into the world. I couldn't believe how radically and instantly priorities can change in a person's life.

I held her immediately after her mom birthed her, just her and I sitting there in the hospital room. When her little eyes locked on mine, I made her a promise—that I would always love her unconditionally.

It was that day that *special love* was created. My kids always ask me what I mean by that phrase and what the secret is to *special love*. I have always told them that one day, I would tell them the answer and the secret. Well, here it is:

*To love, provide, protect, listen—whatever it takes to
enable and equip them with every ounce of energy and
loving acceptance that a human can give another.*

In preparation for writing this book, I asked Katie to share some memorable moments of her childhood, and she said the following:

*When I was a child, my dad had this phrase that he used a lot with
me: special love. It could be something as simple as misplacing my
basketball before practice. Dad would find it seemingly out of thin
air, and I would be in awe. I would ask him how he found it, and
he would say, "It's special love." I know this sounds crazy, but I
found a sense of both safety and magic in those words. Special love
was the foundation of my childhood, and I will cherish it forever.*

In spite of many failures along the way, I've attempted to give that special love to my children with as much vigor and passion as I have, with few exceptions.

My daughter was and is always full of energy and laughter. When her mom and I would take her on walks through the neighborhood, she was always trying to escape the confines of the stroller. I think at age two, she ended up pushing us half the way!

I think she came out of the womb playing sports, a passion of hers for sure. On her first soccer game ever at age fourteen, she scored six goals. The coach approached her mom and I after the game and tried to persuade us to enter her into the Junior Olympics.

Although she excelled at every sport she played, basketball was her game. It seems like not long after she started walking, she and I would spend hours and hours in the backyard shooting hoops. Her playing ability always exceeded my coaching ability, but I still gave it a shot by coaching her teams: the Bumblebees, the rec teams in

Charlotte, and the Carolina Cougars. She advanced her skills to the point that at age eight, she was invited to join an Amateur Athletic Union (AAU) basketball team in Statesville, North Carolina. At that point, I turned her over to Todd Jones, head coach for the AAU Carolina Angels, who was not only a great coach but, more importantly, a wonderful human being. Todd taught the girls strong basketball skills, but more than anything else, he taught them about life. He fought his battle with cancer with tremendous vigor and courage but went home to be with the God he loved on March 13, 2017.

As she grew into a teenager, Katie, who will forever be known to me as "Bug," continued her passionate pursuit of basketball. She would become one of the top basketball players in the state, so good that as a middle schooler, she was playing at the high school level. Although she was too young to be officially recruited, in eighth grade she received scholarship inquiries from Tennessee, UCONN, and UNC. She led in scoring and assists on every team on which she played. Coaches, players, and fans would come from all over to see her play—she was truly brilliant. She was destined for a full ride to a top university—it was only a matter of which offer she would take.

When she wasn't playing on a competitive court, she was playing basketball with the neighborhood kids—except she never played with the girls. There was no competition there. At age ten, she was already playing the high school boys in the neighborhood and beating them consistently. The boys in the neighborhood would get so incredibly frustrated because none of them could ever beat her in basketball; she would just spank them. She was a tough cookie and a fierce competitor. That determination has served her well in business to this day.

Her teams on several occasions advanced to the national championships. Those tournaments were played all over the country—Orlando, New Orleans, Amarillo, Dayton—always accompanied by my parents. We had great times as a family on those trips. On one occasion during the national championship in New Orleans, a cabdriver offered these three tips while driving the dads to the French Quarter: "If you drop a quarter, don't pick it up; don't go past the eight-hundred block; and don't pet the cop's horse." I've never been entirely sure of what he meant, but we followed his advice and had a great time. So good advice for sure.

Bug, her mom, brother Charles, and I were all in this together. Her practices were long and hard and required her mom and I to make three trips a week to Asheville, North Carolina, an hour away from our home for practice. Some of the friendships built during the AAU years will last forever. As Winston Churchill once said, "If you're going through hell, keep going." The journey bonds people together. Faith, family, and friends were principles her mom and I taught our children.

I love Bug's childhood. From the date days that she and I would have, to her wearing my beeper at age four while playing my secretary, we had really wonderful times together. Every note she has ever written to me, I have kept. Some are real tearjerkers!

Her mom and I were very fortunate and both very focused on living debt free, and it was a lesson that also caught on with Bug. On her eighteenth birthday, July 18, 2007, I assembled the family to my office upstairs in the home. I had prearranged a call with my bank to find out the payoff amount for the mortgage on the house—a very large amount. We were all on speakerphone, and on my prompt, I instructed the banker to transfer the full mortgage balance from another account her mom and I had been building. Instantly, the mortgage was paid off, and we were officially debt free. I remain grateful for Dave Ramsey and his teachings on the power of living debt free. It truly is life changing. The grass really does feel better under debt-free toes.

It was actually a special moment for Bug as well. Later, I took her through Dave Ramsey's Financial Peace University, a fundamentals of finance class, and she added that to her list when I asked her to share with me for this book. "Taking a thirteen-week Dave Ramsey Financial Peace class with my dad when I was in high school" was on her list of life's most memorable moments.

Although she received scholarship interest from the University of Tennessee, the University of Connecticut, and the University of North Carolina, Bug's basketball career came to an unfortunate end before she was able to accept any of the offers.

On June 1, 2003, when she was fourteen, she was playing in a tournament in Asheville, North Carolina. She was the starting point guard for the AAU team, and as she was coming down the court, she made a simple quick move to the right when suddenly—snap! With an excruciating noise that echoed throughout the auditorium, she injured her right anterior cruciate ligament (ACL), and down she went. She was able to come back from the injury and keep playing, but on September 11, 2004, she snapped her left ACL during play. Six months later, she snapped her right ACL again. We ran out onto the court to provide aid, but it was too late. When she was able to limp off the court, she hit the wall with her hand and said, "Dad, it's over." Physically and emotionally, she was through with basketball. It was so traumatic that she would tell me later that hearing the squeaks of the sneakers in a basketball gym would bring her to tears.

To this day, I am still so proud of how she handled the loss of a dream with courage and redirected passion. I think her understanding of God's grace from the age of fourteen carried her and sustained her through this very difficult chapter of life.

After basketball, Bug turned up her pursuit of academic success and graduated from Furman University in 2011. Even though my parents never had the opportunity to go to college, I will always be incredibly grateful for the very generous gift of sending Bug to an academic institution like Furman University, referred to as "the Harvard of the South." She had been pursued by the university to play basketball even after her injuries, and it was a good day when she received her letter of acceptance from FU.

For their twenty-first birthdays, I treated each of my kids with a gift, a trip for their special occasion. Katie chose Boston. We had such a wonderful time in spite of almost getting run over by John Kerry and his wife, Theresa, at an intersection in Beacon Hill. We topped the trip off with a beautiful dinner and dancing at the incredible Top of the Hub restaurant in downtown Boston with amazing views of the city and an incredible jazz band that provided us cool tunes to dance to. She sure did look beautiful.

I'm so proud of the woman my daughter has become. She is in a wonderful place in life with business and love. She recently ranked number two out of 120 salespeople in her company. I could write a whole book on her passion for life and her real and raw transparent pursuit of life. Her intelligent creativity and character are beyond words. I've seen her talents, skills, and gifts touch countless people and jobs and relationships her whole life.

I didn't think our relationship and bond could get any stronger, but it did on Thanksgiving evening 2015. After dinner that night, as we sat on the couch, I could tell she had something very heavy on her mind.

She would go on to tell me that after years of struggling with her sexuality, she was gay. We cried together for hours as the bondage and shackles came ripping off of my beautiful daughter. In the twisted form of misguided southern religiosity, she had become so incredibly depressed with an almost unbearable level of shame and guilt. I can't express my level of guilt in so many years of being an asshole fundamentalist that only heaped additional guilt and shame upon her and, I'm sure, countless others.

I can only hope that my daughter, myself, and others will continue to realize that God just loves us for who we are, period. Largely the "churched" community has caused a lot of hurt for some of God's beautiful people.

Sweetie, continue to stand firm in your faith, family, and friendships. You are truly loved beyond measure.

MY SECOND GIFT

"All right, Chuck, you've been dying to tell someone; let me have it."

The anesthesiologist had heard of my staunch stance on not telling anyone—I mean anyone—that I was having a son. His mom refused to be told the gender upfront—even as she carried him—but I chose to find out, unlike I did with my daughter. As the doc and I stood in the hallway, just the two of us, I finally confided in him: "Doc, I'm having a son!"

After an emotional few minutes, he said, "Well, let's go get that boy."

That was truly one of the hardest secrets I've ever had to keep. I was bribed and threatened by family and friends to reveal the secret, but I never caved with any of them. One time, I was on a shuttle bus on route to a PGA event when a stranger from Houston sat beside me. For a minute, I thought, *Surely I can tell this guy.* But the more I thought about it, the more I thought this dude would meet somebody on the golf course that day and tell them, "Hey, I just met the nicest guy on the ride over, and guess what? He's having a boy." I guess I don't run low on paranoia.

It was a miracle that my son, Charles—"Charlie Brown," my nickname for him, or CB for short—didn't die at the hands of his rambunctious sister. He has been tough since the crib. CB as a child in his car seat would frequently ride in silence with his thumb safely planted in his mouth, always thinking. He has always been ahead of his years in wisdom and discernment. Our country is damn fortunate to have my son now serve in a strategic role in the US Army.

There's nothing more important than the gifts and inspiration I've been given from my children

When he was a little guy, CB and I played cowboys and Indians all the time, killing all sorts of imaginary bad guys. After each battle, he would plead, "Daddy, just one more time?"

I was raised on the philosophy "work hard, play hard." I was determined to teach my boy that same principle. When he was still very young, only five years old, he helped me clear the land for our new home. He was such a cute little dude helping me clear out tree after tree, branch after branch. Later, we built a tree house in the woods on our property.

On Father's Day, Charles wrote in a letter to me, "Daddy, thank you for giving me the tools for life … and for my tree house." On his twenty-fourth birthday, I asked him if he remembered that note. He said, "No, Dad, I don't, but I would say the same thing today."

For me, that note is a reminder that there's nothing more important than the gifts and inspiration I've been given from my children. It's a reminder of the things that are most important. But I carry that note in my portfolio, and I use it in every speech I give around the world. I use it in a number of ways to illustrate a point, either motivational, inspirational, or instructional. My goal is to give my audience the tools to help them be better in life and in business. In that way, the impact my son has had on me and countless others is incredible.

My son has always been a tough guy, yet incredibly patient for a dude. I can't count the number of trips he and I made to Lowe's in the building of our family home. I think, even now, he breaks out in a sweat every time the name Lowe's comes up.

I admire my son's work ethic, something that I was determined to teach him. So I had him work on Jason Daniel's tobacco farm at age sixteen. As he has said, "My dad threw me into the farming business"; it was a life-changing experience for sure. When my dad retired, Jason took over much of the property and continued to grow tobacco, so Charles was working some of the same land that I had worked as a young man, and even years later, the processes were very similar. When we picked him up at the end of the summer, Charles had about 3 percent body fat and a deep, dark tan because, like I had all those years earlier, he had spent about fourteen hours a day in the tobacco field all summer long.

My son's work ethic also brought him a lot of success in high school sports, where he played and excelled in soccer, basketball, and baseball. Charles was always well rounded in sports, academics, and social endeavors. In his senior year at Wade Hampton High School, he was tapped as Mr. Wade Hampton. I, his mom, and my parents cheered him on with great enthusiasm as he won the award. My parents always made the four-hour drive to be part of everything my kids did.

As I did with my daughter, I also taught Charles to excel at everything and be comfortable with anything—boiler room or boardroom, sitting at the opera in a tux or drinking beer and wearing flip-flops and shorts at a bluegrass event. In other words, I wanted them to have range. Range is really important to me. I wanted my kids to be accepting of the janitor, the CEO, and everyone in between and to be comfortable and conversant in every situation.

That quest to help Charles have range took him and me on one of the most memorable trips ever. We sailed out of Hubbard's Marina in Saint Petersburg, Florida, for a one-hundred-mile, three-day fishing trip along with thirty-one other men we had just met and Tammy, the ship's cook. God forbid I should ever get in a bar fight, but if I did, I would want Tammy on my side. As I approached her on the first night of the trip to ask about dinner, I found her in the galley of the ship, braless and with a cigarette dangling from her mouth. I asked, "Hey, Tammy, when is dinner?"

Her reply: "When I'm damn well ready to cook it." I didn't ask again during the duration of the trip. It was a crazy trip where we would sleep twenty minutes at a time while we fished, literally around the clock. We returned to shore three days later, having not showered and really smelling like fish. What a beautiful trip!

On one occasion, right before Charles would leave home to start college, he had a small situation involving a traffic citation, as many young adults do. During Charles's time on the docket, the judge asked Charles if he had a parent in the courtroom. As I approached the bench, the judged asked, "Mr. Crumpton, what can you tell me about your son?"

I said the first thing that came to my mind, and I would say it again today: "Your honor, if I were ever held captive in an Afghan prison and needed a rescue, I can't even think of a second person I would call."

The judge said, as he closed the file, "That's all I need to hear. Son, you have a very bright future ahead of you. Citation dismissed."

In June 2014, Charles and I had the privilege to drive across the country from Greenville, South Carolina, to San Diego, California, where he would continue his college education. I hate to drive, and I've developed a crazy adult-onset fear of heights while driving across tall bridges or over mountains. As much as I dreaded driving nearly three thousand miles, I was excited to spend time with my son. The trip took six days and six nights, and I wished it could've lasted sixty days. We made some incredible memories along the trip, including great barbecue in Memphis, CrossFit in Dallas, and incredibly warm and sacrificial hospitality from my friend Sergio in El Paso.

There was also a little law enforcement skirmish in Odessa, Texas. Charles was napping, and I was driving his very comfortable black luxury sedan with blacked-out windows, a car he had bought from my dad. It was four o'clock in the afternoon in west Texas, and I was hauling ass at just over one hundred miles an hour, no other cars on the flat, barren road. Out of nowhere, a Texas Mountie approached from the bramblebush. Assured I was Pablo Escobar, he was terribly disappointed when I emerged from Charles's car wearing gym shorts and a pink CrossFit T-shirt. I was sure I would either get a $2,000 fine or execution on the spot. To my great surprise and gratitude, he let me go with a warning ticket and a verbal admonition: "Slow it down, boy, when you drive through my state." *Yes, sir.*

On the last day of the trip, as we drove through the sun-blessed rock and stone of Arizona, I had tears streaming down my face as I listened to the country song on the radio from the Zac Brown Band, "Toes," which repeats the line "Life is good today." I realized that this was a once-in-a-lifetime opportunity with my son, one that I would cherish forever.

As I did with my daughter, I had the chance to celebrate Charles's twenty-first birthday with a trip. I chose New York City for him because he had never been there before. His sister and I, along with Charles, had been terribly disappointed the night before when, on his actual birthday, he was not carded when ordering his first legal adult beverage. Of all places, that changed when we rolled up into the Big Apple. After seeing sights all over New York, we attended his first Yankees game. As we approached the stadium, the bottom dropped out of the sky, and it poured rain like crazy. I literally prayed, "Lord, please dry up the rain."

After an hour of rain delay, we were on. C. C. Sabathia was the starting pitcher, and Alex Rodriguez was batting cleanup. Later, Rodriguez would smack a grand slam over the left-field wall. As we got settled in, I told Charles we had to have a beer and a brat at Yankee Stadium. When Charles ordered his first beer and hot dog, the server said, "Son, I'll have to see your ID." *Yes!* His first time carded was actually at Yankee Stadium. The trip to Yankee Stadium was eerily similar to my amazing first trip to Yankee Stadium when my dad took me (age twelve) and my brother (age seven) there. That night, Reggie Jackson hammered a grand slam over the left-field wall to give me my first-ever MLB home-run experience.

After a crazy close game, we were off to our next stop on the tour—a midnight reservation at the infamous PDT bar (Please Don't Tell), the original speakeasy bar in New York City. Only with a reservation do you enter a telephone booth in a run-down hot dog stand. When you enter the phone booth, you pick up the receiver and give them your last name. A revolving door opens to a top-notch, first-class bar with amazing specialty cocktails. We sat, drank, laughed, and talked until nearly three o'clock in the morning.

Perhaps the most moving stop on our New York trip was the Ground Zero memorial. I remember being awestruck, not only at the memorial itself—God bless the victims and their loved ones—but at the sight of my son viewing it. As my many pictures would indicate, I viewed the site of this enormous tragedy and unparalleled patriotism through the eyes of my future-soldier son. The three-day trip was filled with wonder, amazement, and tons of activity. I think we slept a total of six hours the whole time.

We survived the trip, and Charles went on to crush his college career. He graduated from San Diego State University on May 11, 2018, with high honors and a near-perfect grade point average after obtaining his fluency in Arabic. His academic success, along with his language proficiency, would later help him earn the prestigious Clinton Scholarship for foreign study in Dubai, a full scholarship granted to ten recipients each year out of a thousand applicants. Perhaps saying I'm proud of my son would be a slight understatement.

At the time I was writing this chapter, I had just finished hosting my son at my house for two weeks. It was a gift I will never forget. As the stress for him of getting his stuff moved from San Diego wore on through the two weeks, we had the opportunity to spend one afternoon riding bikes around Seabrook Island near Charleston. This had been one of our happy places as the kids were growing up. After a relaxing bike ride around the island, we stopped for a beer at the Ryder Cup Bar at the Ocean Course. As a father, you live for moments like this when your child says, "Dad, you've always been my dad, but you've become my best friend."

No car, house, pool, bank account, career, or award can ever compete with those words.

CHAPTER 6

NEVER THOUGHT IT WOULD HAPPEN TO ME

It came out of nowhere. The call was from Peter T. Loftin, founder and CEO of Business Telecom Inc. (BTI). BTI was a medium-sized telecommunications/data technology company with about six hundred employees, based in Raleigh, North Carolina. Peter (Pete) founded the company in 1984, after overhearing some executives from the telecommunications industry discuss the breakup of AT&T during a lunch at a local hotel in Raleigh while he was waiting tables as a server.

He wanted to get in and grab a piece of what surely would become a massive spin-off industry. Under Pete's creative, infectious, and renegade leadership, the company was thriving, but some of the regions were struggling in the midst of rapid company growth.

"Chuck, Pete Loftin. I've heard great things about you in the market. I want you to join our team as regional manager in Greensboro." Wow, my first management job! At the time, I was at the top of my game as a major account manager at the company where I had worked for my mentor, Leighton "Cub" Cubbage. But I wanted to tackle management.

BTI did not have the best image or reputation in the market-place, but I felt I could be a change agent. I felt strongly that I could manage folks and make a difference based on the leadership princi-ples I had learned from my dad and the servant-leadership mentoring from Cub.

My first meeting with Pete after being hired was a bit awkward. Pete began by going through the roster of employees in the Greens-boro office, with editorial on each one. After the first employee was discussed—someone whom he wanted me to fire immediately—I said, "Pete, you hired me to run this branch, and that's what I'm going to do. With all due respect, I'll make my own decisions on personnel without input from anyone."

That was the first day of what would turn out to be a very inter-esting ride.

WHAT HAVE I GOTTEN MYSELF INTO?

I took the job, but as I walked into the run-down, dumpy, outdated office with broken chairs and taped-up desks, I thought, *What have I gotten myself into?* I had just left a beautiful office, a good salary, and a great company with a strong reputation in the marketplace. I had built strong momentum and stellar sales success with my previous company, and I had been on the path to make a lot of money.

Now, I was inheriting a young, inexperienced bunch of sales and support people who were desperately struggling in their jobs, not because they lacked raw talent, but because they had no leadership or daily direction. I would soon love and lead and try to rescue these folks from being at rock bottom, the last-place branch in the company out of ten branches. That was May 1, 1989.

As I had learned from Cub, I wanted to set a good example for my folks. I was the first one to arrive in the office that first day. As my team trickled in, we exchanged a few pleasantries, then got down to business. I brought each one individually into my office and asked them one simple question: "Do you want to be successful?"

I received a plethora of different answers that day, only one that really surprised me. An employee I'll call "CD" said to me, "No, I can't see myself being managed with such accountability." We shook hands and packed his belongings, and I wished him well in his new endeavors as the door on the elevator closed.

My next meeting was with Shepard Hayes, a charismatic, good-looking dude who had been a great high school football player, averaging nearly three hundred yards per game as a standout running back. He would leave football in his rearview mirror in high school and go on to become a cheerleader at East Carolina University. That meeting with him on that beautiful spring day would change both of our lives forever.

I started the meeting by asking the same question I asked of the others. "Shepard, do you want to be successful?" Looking back after all these years, I was not surprised by his answer.

"With everything I have," he replied.

I said, "Okay, great. If you do everything I tell you to do, you will be successful, perhaps even the best salesperson in the company."

Every company, family, and organization can only have one chief. For good or bad, I would be his chief, and he would be my soldier. As my dad told me when I was an arrogant twelve-year-old pissant, "You do the doing; I do the thinking." Success starts with getting your mind right and by implementing fundamentals of attitude and activity, the building blocks of success.

I told Shepard that we would start the next morning at seven thirty sharp in the conference room and left him with, "By the way, you have to wear a suit to work; sport coats are not allowed." I had learned that lesson from Cub and Bud Stoner—you have to look good in order to be good.

The next morning, Shepard showed up at 7:45-ish, wearing slacks, no tie, and a sport coat. I would not allow him into the conference room. He stormed out and was headed toward home when he slammed on the brakes of his car and said to himself, *I'll be damned if that SOB is going to stop me.* He made a U-turn, went to the Men's Wearhouse, and bought three new suits.

He was in the office the next morning, well before seven thirty, and he said to me, "Let's go to work, boss." To the letter of the law, Shepard incorporated every single procedure and policy I required of my salespeople. It was a proven, successful formula that, if implemented on a daily, weekly, monthly basis consistently, would make a person successful.

By November of that year, at our annual meeting, six months after our meeting of the minds on day one, Shepard was recognized by Peter Loftin, CEO of BTI, as the top company salesperson of the year. Shepard's humility, passion to win, and incredible work ethic had taken him from last place in the company, with a target on his back, to first place.

Sitting in the back of that large banquet hall, I was so proud of Shepard as he confidently approached the podium and received the most prestigious award in the company. Shepard had not only become one of my dearest friends on earth and a trusted and competent professional, but also a standard for all the employees in the company and many in the industry.

Some years later, a phone call would rip my heart out.

The call came in at 7:57 p.m. on June 9, 2015. I had just walked in the front door of my home after having drinks and dinner with my best friend. When I answered the phone, I heard the voice of Shepard's beloved brother Floyd. "Chuck," he said, "I hate to tell you this, but Shepard passed away last night in his sleep. The family and I would like for you to deliver his eulogy."

After hearing those words, I stood there speechless. Shepard was only fifty-one years old when he had a massive heart attack in his sleep. Three days later, on a one-hundred-degree day at a packed, standing-room-only Godwin Baptist Church in Lumberton, North Carolina, I would share fond, funny, and beautiful memories of my dear friend. God broke the mold when he made this incredibly special, loving, kind, generous, and loyal friend.

BIGGER, BETTER THINGS

"When I reach my hand in the basket, I want to always grab a wing," Pete Loftin would say to the server at J. P. Looney's restaurant as he visited our office in Greensboro one day. Our region had gone from last place in the company to first place. Pete had stopped by to congratulate the team on our success. I was incredibly blessed to have a team like that, one that had rallied together and overcome a mountain of odds.

Doing so had made it possible for us to move out of that shithole office. I negotiated and designed a new office just across the street, a beautiful one with nice, new furniture. We were rocking—except for one thing. In spite of the tremendous sales success we were having, my folks were struggling to win deals against our largest competitor, the company I had left a year earlier to rebuild this team. I called all the sales employees in my office one afternoon and asked them to close the door. On speakerphone, I dialed the district manager from the company I had left.

After a few pleasantries were exchanged, I said, "Jerry, I want to challenge you to a sales contest. Your team against mine. You name the rules and the stakes, but let's rock 'n' roll."

After what seemed to be endless silence, he said, "Chuck, I don't think so." My team stood there in silence before breaking out in a cheer. From that day on, we rarely lost a deal to them in a head-to-head battle. My folks were buoyed with the eye of the tiger.

We would not have been so successful without my team, which included Rich Miller, Leslie, Mark, Kathleen, Stephanie, and others. Everyone from my little posse from 1989 would go on to bigger and better things, in life and business. Thirty years later, I still stay in touch with some of them and remain very proud of the small role I played in their success. I encourage you to find someone in your life today. Then love on them, encourage them, and join them on their journey of success.

As wild, eccentric, and ostentatious as Pete Loftin was, I knew him as a generous man who took life and business very personally. I witnessed his meteoric rise as an entrepreneur, from nothing to building a multimillion-dollar telecommunications company to one day owning Versace Mansion in South Beach. On the company trip that I won for being top regional manager in 1990, Pete personally took care of my six-month-old baby girl, renting my little family a private limo from the airport along with a private villa while celebrating in a five-star resort in the Bahamas.

As I sat there with Pete in that restaurant in Greensboro, he asked me to move to Charlotte and take over the struggling regional office one hundred miles to the south. The region was in last place in the company and losing thousands of dollars each week. I said to Pete, "I'll take the job in Charlotte, if I can bring Rich Miller with me." Along with my wife and baby girl, I loaded up a U-Haul and left for the Queen City—and so did Rich.

To the chagrin of some of my folks in Charlotte, I implemented the exact same program we had in place in Greensboro. Great attitude, high activity, extreme integrity, and professional business-development practices that even included changing how we answered the phone. The devil is in the details, and it's always the details that make the biggest difference in the long run. We slowly rebuilt the team with people who looked and walked the part.

Dawn L. would not have been my first choice as my newest hire in Charlotte. She had been referred to me by a trusted coworker, but I honestly felt like she couldn't sell herself out of a wet paper bag. She was kind, yet unpolished. Since I felt almost obligated to hire her, I thought the best solution was to put up so many roadblocks during the interview process that she would just get frustrated with the process and go home. After multiple interviews, where I had her sell me everything from pencils to the wallpaper, basically just trying to talk her and myself out of the hire, I finally gave her a chance. Since it was obvious that she didn't have the natural talent that so many on the team had, I told her, "Dawn, you're just going to have to outwork everyone on this team to make it."

Did she ever! One of the first ones in the office every morning, she knocked on more doors than anyone in the company and would return to the office at the end of each day exhausted but victorious. The legendary coach Vince Lombardi once said, "I firmly believe that any man's finest hours—his greatest fulfillment to all he holds dear—is that moment when he has worked his heart out in good cause and lies exhausted on the field of battle—victorious."[2] Dawn never made it to be number one, but to this day, she remains one of my top role models characterizing determination, work ethic, and a can-do spirit.

In less than a year, Charlotte had become the number one region in the company. You put a solid process in place and hire good people, and magic will happen.

AN ITCH, THEN A SCRATCH— NOT OF MY OWN MAKING

I began to get the itch to do something on my own. On a routine visit to the BTI corporate offices in Raleigh, I had the chance to sit down with Richard Brown, CFO, to review some P&L information. As we were wrapping up the meeting, I mentioned to Richard that at some point in the future I wanted to start my own business, perhaps in some kind of partnership with BTI. He asked my permission to share my thoughts with Pete, to which I gladly agreed. I had rebuilt two very successful regions and felt like this could be a great partnership between myself and the company in the future. That was late afternoon on Wednesday.

---

2   "Famous Quotes by Vince Lombardi," *Vince Lombardi*, accessed June 5, 2019, http://www.vincelombardi.com/quotes.html.

The call on Friday morning from my boss came as a shock. "I want to stop by and say hello," he said. No one that sits in an office 166 miles away stops by to say hello.

I hung up the phone and called my wife. "I'm getting fired," I told her.

When my boss walked in my office three hours later, he couldn't look me in the eyes, but he said, "We have decided to let you go." I'm assuming that someone who takes things very personally had felt abandoned by my announcement. I boxed my personal items, hugged my team members goodbye, and made the incredibly long and lonely twenty-five-minute drive to my home near Lake Norman.

As I walked in the door that afternoon in May, I faced my wife, a stay-at-home mom, and my baby girl, then three years old. I never thought it would happen to me—I never thought I would be let go from a position, much less let go so abruptly after so much success.

The feelings of failure, loss, stress, and resentment were overwhelming. My close neighbors included executives from Duke Power and Caterpillar, and I was embarrassed to face them and the others that night at our weekly cul-de-sac cookout. How had I gone from making the company millions of dollars and being the golden boy of management to being fired? I was the first one in the office and the last one to leave. I had stood in the trench for my people and had called on them to climb the mountain with me. Where were my people? Where was my mountain? I had charged both markets like charging hell with a water pistol. I had been rewarded and awarded. I had plaques and trophies to tell the world how great I was. Where were the cheers and accolades now? It would be the first backward step in my nonperfect journey.

I made a decision that day that if I ever managed anyone again, I would make it a policy to never fire someone on a Friday afternoon.

There's not a damn thing one can do at four o'clock on a Friday afternoon but suffer through the weekend with misery and loss. I've honored that promise with the hundreds and hundreds of employees I've hired and managed in the more than twenty-eight years since.

> **When one door closes, another door opens, but the hallway in between may suck**

It was a shitty weekend. When one door closes, another door opens, but the hallway in between may suck. Faced with a large mortgage, two car payments, a stay-home wife, and a baby who really liked to eat, I knew I had to make some changes. We decided to sell the house but thought we would start by selling the really cool hot tub that was off the back deck. We needed the money to repaint the house. I ran an ad in *The Charlotte Observer*, the local newspaper, and within minutes of the ad hitting, my phone rang. Howard, a local Realtor who had just moved from New York City and whom I'd never met, was calling to inquire about the hot tub and asked why I was selling it. I told him I was preparing to sell the house. He immediately said, "Tell me about your house."

"I'm not asking you to sell my house," I snapped.

He snapped right back, "If you'll shut your mouth, I'll tell you what the deal is."

What? I was taken aback by someone who would quickly become my new ally. Howard was an obnoxious Realtor who, at that moment, was dancing on my last nerve. He went on to get details about the house, never having been to my neighborhood before. He then said, "Perfect. I'll have the buyer there tomorrow at ten a.m."

Yeah, right, I thought. But the next morning, promptly at ten, the doorbell rang. At that point, I was convinced that Howard was a nutcase, but I overcame my concern and opened the door anyway.

Turns out, our home was perfect for one of Howard's clients, a newly retired executive from Detroit. She made a full cash offer (plus Howard's commission), and we closed in three weeks. God was looking out for my little family.

THE BEST DAMNED TAP DANCE

The next couple of years were filled with good old-fashioned hard work and incredible opportunities. The bills had to be paid, and finances were tight, but I never missed a payment on anything. (I could write a book just on that chapter of my life alone.)

In my little business as a technology consultant, jobs came in from everywhere. To my great surprise, I was awarded the bid to become the official telecommunications consultant for a county/government health system in North Carolina. Alvin

Take care of the people who join you on your journey, and they will take care of you.

Tyndall would be my client contact on the project, but he would soon become my friend. For nine years I would serve Alvin and the organization, which helped me grow personally and professionally.

I performed my tasks as a consultant well, but I learned a lot about life and business in the process. I remain very grateful for those years and often reflect on the many wonderful and thought-provoking conversations Alvin and I enjoyed. Alvin and I were on polar opposites of social and political issues, but we would go to lunch and debate for hours on everything from sexuality to social reform to politics, whatever. Each of those conversations got me to questioning why I believe what I believe and to understanding why I take the positions I take. Not that I was always right, nor was he, but the debates made me think. He was just a brilliant person who challenged me in every area. Take care of the people who join you on your journey, and they will take care of you.

In 1995, this whole "Internet thing" was rocking and rolling, and I was tasked—as either the subject matter expert on the Internet or the loudest mouth in the industry—to deliver the first public speech on the subject of the Internet at the Chamber of Commerce function in Greenville, South Carolina.

What was supposed to be a crowd of fifty turned out to be a swelling of over two hundred people, standing room only. As the crowd that morning became more and more worked up, I was pumped and ready to share a well-prepared PowerPoint on the hottest technology to hit our generation. As I walked up to the podium after being introduced by the president of the chamber, I noticed my audiovisual guy whispering the words that only I, but not the audience, could see and hear: "It's not working." The laptop hosting my ninety-minute presentation had crashed.

For the next hour, I tried desperately to say in words what could have been much better articulated through the graphics of the slide deck. As I walked off stage, David Brown, president of the chamber, said to me privately, "That's the best damned tap dance I've ever seen."

The crowd cheered and was appreciative. It all worked out. If you've never had a presentation go to hell in a handbasket, hang on—it probably will. Know your material and connect with your audience, and they will join you on the journey.

ONE LAST GO

It was an offer I could not turn down. My little family had now grown to four, with the addition of my son a few months earlier. The salary of $167,000 plus bonuses, with great healthcare benefits, would serve my young family well. MCI telecommunications (now Verizon), a Fortune 25 company, would be my new home. My office was on the fiftieth floor of the Bank of America headquarters building in downtown Charlotte. From my office I could see down into the Carolina Panthers football stadium. The company had a lavish travel and entertainment policy and encouraged employees who traveled for business to eat and drink well. They believed if you were sacrificing your family for business, spare no expense.

In my first year, the company spent nearly $3 million on one management meeting in Dallas, where Huey Lewis entertained us in the midst of a lavish indoor fireworks celebration. Private jets and limos typically carried around senior managers and above. The company spent a fortune but was making a killing in the marketplace. I was in the division that managed major and national accounts, Fortune 500 companies with large complex data networks. Again, I was blessed to have a great team of people. We worked hard and played hard and enjoyed a lot of success. The idea of such lavish spending was foreign and a bit uncomfortable for me.

When I first rolled on the scene, the company had a deafening attrition in its sales ranks of several thousand sales professionals. Seventy-three percent of the account managers, hired at an average salary of $60,000 plus commission, were bailing in their first ninety days. If you do the math, the company was hemorrhaging to the tune of millions per year. A small team of senior managers from around the United States, including me, went to work on the problem and ended up developing the first-in-industry branch sales development method (BSDM) manual. It was a published day-by-day, step-by-step manual for the first 160 days of a new hire's life. It was very detailed on exactly what to do every day. A clear and easy track to run on. In developing the program, I implemented many of the ideas I used in building my two successful regions at BTI and my personal sales career earlier. The program turned out to be a huge success, and the company saw attrition fall to 18 percent in the first year of deployment.

As the company continued to do well, it became the target for the world's biggest corporate acquisition. WorldCom purchased the company in 1998 for $37 billion in cash. Bernie Ebbers, the Canadian cowboy CEO of WorldCom, would later say to a large group of MCI managers assembled in Louisville, "Look at the person to your right and to the person on your left. Chances are, they won't be here next year." There was a new sheriff in town. Leading up to the acquisition, the belt had started tightening. After it, jets were grounded, and limos were sold.

My family had just bought a new home in the Lake Norman area, near Charlotte. It was a beautiful home that I had spotted by driving around the area looking for a new, larger place for my family. I called the number on the for-sale-by-owner sign in the front yard and made an appointment to see the house later that evening. As the door opened, I was shocked to see the homeowners, my friend Bill and his wife, standing in the doorway. Bill had been a coworker of mine, but we had lost contact with each other. After I toured the house and fell in love with it, Bill and I drove down to the local McDonald's and wrote the contract on a napkin. We closed on the house thirty days later.

We had purchased the home earlier that month, even after hearing rumors of layoffs and employee changes coming, because I went to my boss, CJ, for assurance of my good standing on the senior leadership team. He looked at me and said, "Chuck, what are you worried for? You're doing a great job for the company. Relax and go buy that house."

A few weeks later, we had a different conversation. CJ would go on to say, "Chuck, I'm sorry to tell you, your position is being moved to Atlanta," one of the corporate headquarters sites. Again, I'd never thought it would happen to me.

Refusing to accept the transfer to Atlanta. I went to my office at my new home—the home with a huge mortgage—and made a list. It was the list of every person I had known and worked with during my twelve years in the telecommunications industry. When your back is against the wall, you do what you have to do.

The list of friends was long, and the calls were encouraging. I had made a lot of good contacts and close friends and had enjoyed high respect among my peers, but enough was enough.

CHAPTER 7

ENOUGH IS ENOUGH

I t was a long fall from the fiftieth floor to the toolshed. Located in one corner of my garage, the toolshed was packed with shovels, rakes and hoes, and a lot of dust and dirt.

In the days that followed my decision to leave MCI, I extensively pondered what to do next. Before pulling the final trigger on doing my own thing, I was contacted by a recruiter for a vice president's role at a large computer software company located in the southeastern United States. I was impressed with the company and decided to work through the interview process.

On the fifth and final interview, I waited in the boardroom for the CEO to arrive. The door opened, and a very distinguished, well-dressed older gentleman walked in and introduced himself. He looked at me in silence for what seemed like hours and then finally asked the only question of the interview: "Chuck, have you had enough failure in your life to know what success really is?" Wow! Ponder that for a moment.

Apparently, I had the right answer, and we left for lunch, where I was given the job offer with a great salary and benefits that included paid private schools for my children. It was a tough offer to turn down, but I did.

I put on my big-boy britches and went home to the toolshed. After taking all the yard tools out, I put a tiny desk and a small chair in there so that I could go to work. The little room seemed closed in and cramped, so I went out and bought a mirror to hang on the wall right above my desk. It made my little fifty-square-foot world headquarters seem much larger and more open. The next purchase was a small window-unit air conditioner so I wouldn't die from heat exhaustion.

On that first day of being self-employed, I had to figure it out and figure it out fast. Later that morning, I picked up the phone and dialed my first number for business-development purposes. It would be the first of thousands of calls I would make to build my business.

The office setup worked pretty well until my retired eighty-two-year-old neighbor across the street mowed his grass using a run-down lawn mower with no muffler. Four times a week he was out there, and with all that racket going on, I had to shut the door of the toolshed. Since the air conditioner blew right in my ear, I also had to shut it off while making phone calls. With my right hand, I would dial and wait for an answer, and with my left hand I would shut off the unit. It was a slightly different setting than the fiftieth-floor, mahogany-and-granite office I had left behind.

But it was the best decision of my life.

BOOM–AND BUST

I decided on day one of my business that the company would be built on these principles:

1. To treat everyone the way I wanted to be treated

2. To always do what I said I would do

3. To have the highest level of integrity in all business ethics, especially when it came to money

I had built a strong network of contacts in the telecommunications/technology space, so it made sense to start there. I knew how to recruit talent and build teams, since I had built a successful program at MCI, so I decided I would recruit and place high-level national account managers into roles at large telecommunications companies.

The only problem was that I didn't have any candidates or clients. So I started dialing, figuring that at some point if I had a candidate, I could get a client. Or if I had a client, I could get a candidate.

The call came in one morning from the hundreds of messages I had left for companies and candidates. "This is Reg Brown from Sprint. Who the hell are you, and what do you want?"

I felt like the cow looking at the new gate. "Reg," I told him, "thank you for calling me back. I know the type of talent you're looking for, and if you give me a chance, I promise not to let you down."

An eternity of silence. "What's your fax number? I'll send you a contract."

I had my first client, and we were off to the races.

Reg and I would go on to build a great friendship and business relationship. I would make frequent trips to Atlanta to look him in the eye just to say, "Thanks."

I was doing hundreds of thousands of dollars in the industry, when one day, I noticed a discrepancy with my accounts receivables payments with Sprint. The company had overpaid one of my invoices by $40,000! I immediately picked up the phone and called Reg. "Shit," he said. "I don't know how to handle this. Vendors don't call about overpayments. I'll have to call corporate in Kansas City and see what the hell we do with this."

After a few phone calls to get direction from corporate, Reg asked that I issue a credit to cover the deficit. I mailed a check for $40,000 to Sprint immediately, and we were rocking and rolling again.

I believe God honors strong business integrity, and as a result of being faithful to one of my foundational principles, the business flourished.

I hired several other recruiters to help with the workload. Business was good. We had clients and candidates all over the country, and word was spreading that we were good, could be trusted, and were producing great results with the industry's strongest talent. It was 1999, and my personal income that year would crest $300,000.

Then the dot-com sector blew up.

The ripple effect of the dot-com bust would cause massive layoffs and hiring freezes all over the telecommunications/technology sector. My income in 2000 plummeted to $18,000. The 5,200-square-foot custom home I built on ten acres would be finished on June 1, 2000.

As I finished out that year, I wondered every night how I would be able to make the very large mortgage payment along with the other bills and also feed my family. It was an incredibly stressful time.

I would make the 3,200-foot walk to my mailbox each morning, partially crying and partially praying for an answer to my financial dilemma. On many occasions, I would break down in my solitude, fearing I would lose the house and be considered a failure to my family and

I was a classic entrepreneur— comfortable building new relationships and gifted as a listener.

friends. I knew I had to make a change. The telecommunications industry would take five years to recover, and I knew Duke Power would not accept my IOU note.

I started researching different industries—legal, financial, healthcare, and others—to make a decision on where to build my next business.

What I decided would change my life.

THE BIRTH OF MEDPOINT

In May 2002, Medpoint LLC was born.

I could spell FDA, but I knew very little of the healthcare industry. After massive research and study, what seemed to be an equivalent to going to medical school, I landed on building a firm that would provide specialized expertise in quality assurance and regulatory affairs (QA/RA) for medical device and pharmaceutical companies. I was a classic entrepreneur—comfortable building new relationships and gifted as a listener.

The first client opportunity that came my way was a permanent search project with Fuji Medical in Stamford, Connecticut. The company was part of the worldwide Fuji organization and was in need of a chief quality officer (CQO) in its medical device sector.

Thank goodness it was a C-level position and not a more tactical-level position such as quality engineer (QE).

From my months and months of research, I knew enough about the industry to ask the right questions about the role and to understand the position from a strategic perspective. Had I tried to recruit a QE right out of the gate, I would have died in the weeds.

The retained search contract was for ninety days, and my candidate accepted the offer on day eighty-eight. With a commission well over $30,000, my little healthcare company was successfully launching. Shortly after my CQO started at Fuji, the company asked me to fill a position for vice president of quality and regulatory, which I did within sixty days. I would go on to fill a number of positions for the company, particularly in the QA/RA department.

The early success would allow me to continue to learn the nuts and bolts of regulatory in the healthcare industry as well as put some cash in the bank for financial stability.

THE FOCUS EXPANDED

The next couple of years, I saw a lot of success in the permanent placement part of my business. Companies from all over the United States called asking for help. And I was growing in my technical knowledge as a healthcare professional.

Then the opportunity came that would alter our business model. It was with Johnson & Johnson. Based in New Jersey, J&J is the largest healthcare company in the world with 134,000 employees and $81 billion dollars in revenue.

The company was considering outsourcing some of its projects and was looking for firms that could help augment its internal resources with contract, certified quality-assurance professionals. I thought, *Well, we're doing a good job on the permanent search projects; let's give this short-term contract project a try*. It would also be great to have a company as respected as Johnson & Johnson in our portfolio of clients.

With limited funds in the travel budget, I was on my way to New Jersey. After landing in Newark and renting a car, I drove twenty-three miles in the snow to arrive at the headquarters of one of the operating companies within the massive family of companies at J&J.

As I parked the car and was walking across the parking lot to building ten, my phone rang. It was the administrative assistant to the person I was scheduled to meet with. She told me that my contact would not be able to meet as scheduled due to an emergency that had just come up.

I stood there for a brief moment with the snow up to my shins to ponder my next move. From somewhere deep inside of me, a voice of determination uttered, "I understand. But in all due respect, I have to have this meeting. I'm happy to wait in the lobby as long as it takes."

Everything worked out a bit later in the morning, and the meeting finally happened. It would be the start of a wonderful relationship with the company that has grown year over year since that day in late 2004. As part of this valuable client relationship, we would grow to hire industry professionals all over Europe and Asia, becoming a global consulting company by 2007. The expansion served our customer in reducing large travel costs and fueled us in building a worldwide footprint. We would win an Innovation Award in 2008 for creativity in building solutions and value while reducing costs. Both companies share the pursuit of excellence girded by extreme integrity as our credos would indicate.

BUILDING ON MUTUAL TRUST

As the long-term consulting part of the business began to grow, I found some of my early contractors/consultants through knocking on a lot of doors and asking for referrals. Bob W. and Dawn C. would join my team as I built this new outreach. I am so thankful that these two well-qualified and busy professionals were willing to take a chance on me, someone they had never met.

The words on a contract don't matter if the trust is not there

Bob started working with us after I secured a new project with a large medical-device company in Atlanta. The company had a particularly complex need in the regulatory space, one that matched Bob's credentials perfectly. He was living in the suburbs of Chicago when I called him up and asked him to join me on the project.

I remember the conversation like it was yesterday. Bob asked, "How much are you going to pay me?"

I said, "I think I can pay you X based on my budget."

He said, "Fine. When are you going to pay me?"

I said, "When I get paid."

He said, "Okay, I'm going to trust you." We had no written agreement, no contract, just a simple commitment between two professionals built on a lot of mutual trust.

Due to the travel, food, and hotel costs, Bob would carry an average of $30,000 to $40,000 of expenses on his personal credit card before he was reimbursed by Medpoint. He never missed getting a check from us, and every aspect of the project was completed with excellence, on his part as well as ours. It was a great example of how business should be done—one promise to another built on old-fashioned business ethics.

We have grown up over the years to have complex, detailed agreements between our employees, consultants, and clients. But the foundation is still the same—the words on a contract don't matter if the trust is not there.

Bob is still working with us today.

THE STAKES GET HIGHER

"Our product is being held at the Russian border. Do you have a regulatory expert with FDA credentials who speaks fluent Russian?" The call came from Mike C., the senior VP of QA/RA at a $4 billion medical-device company. That was two o'clock on a Wednesday afternoon, the day after the resume/CV of Tracy O. had floated across my desk from a trusted source.

I told Mike, "I think I can help. Can we schedule a call in forty-five minutes?" I hung up the phone; got Tracy on the line; discussed his background, credentials, and availability; and asked him to join me on the 2:45 p.m. call with Mike, my potential new client.

By 3:15 p.m., thirty minutes into the call, Mike requested Tracy to be on site immediately to deal with the very costly product seizure in Russia. I believe one of the keys to building an excellent company is to respond as fast as possible with competence and care. So within two hours, I had Tracy rebooked from his previous itinerary and scheduled to be on site early Monday morning.

Mike and I agreed to move forward as quickly as possible and had the contract in place within two weeks. Our word was our bond. Tracy did a phenomenal job on the project, and we would go on to serve that company for the next four years with multiple people on site performing a large number of quality, regulatory, and validation projects.

Within two years of the start of the project, we were invoicing this client in eight different locations around the United States with over twenty different Medpoint resources.

Trust was put to the test one day when my accountant approached me and told me about the billing problem. This client had overpaid a stack of invoices from us through four different locations of its accounts payable system. The overpayment amounted to more than $100,000. I immediately called Mike and requested some face time with him over lunch.

After catching up for a few minutes at lunch, Mike conveyed to me he was pressed for time and flying out to the annual board meeting in two hours. I relayed to him the details of the billing issue I had just discovered. Mike leaned back in his chair, took off his glasses, and said, "Chuck, you drove eight hours to tell me this?"

I said, "Mike, my integrity means everything to me. And I wanted to tell you before you found out."

We discussed the root cause of the problem and made action items to ensure the process would be permanently corrected. The credit was systematically issued, and it never happened again. You can't put a price tag on trust.

BUILDING A TEAM

In the early days of building the business, I had to do everything: sell the projects, source the talent, invoice the clients, and pay the consultants. My philosophy in building my business was, "If it's to be, it's up to me." That paradigm I would later find out would not serve me well. I needed like-minded others to make this mission a success.

I recalled the story of Lee Iacocca in the early design phases of the Ford Mustang. On the prompting of Mr. Iacocca to get the convertible to prototype as soon as possible, his team of engineers agreed and told him they could have a prototype in eighteen months. He replied to them, "You don't understand. Cut the top off the damn car, and bring it around to the front of the building."

You do what you have to do, including staying in hotels you don't want to stay in. I didn't have much money for travel and entertainment—unlike my MCI days—so at one point, I negotiated an extremely low rate of fifty-five dollars per night at a scary hotel near one of my clients, which I would call home for the first part of that project. I truly believed the place was haunted. There were several instances of doors opening and closing, money missing, and strange noises in the middle of the night.

The company began to grow quickly, and projects were coming in from all over the world. I could no longer keep up with everything and desperately needed to build a team around the quickly expanding business-development efforts. Processes and procedures were addressed, and the business began to grow in its organizational structure.

One of the first key employees to join the team was Renee. Renee had just graduated from Furman University and was considering Harvard Law School. She interviewed with me and was hired. On her first day of work, she asked me to outline her job responsibilities. I said, "Answer the phones, and file stuff." Later, she told me the phones didn't ring, and we didn't deal with paper. So I told her, "Okay. Go build something that produces revenue." And she did just that and ended up having a great career at Medpoint, where she was personally responsible for excellent service to some of our largest clients. She went well beyond the call of duty, and through great sacrifice, she would go on to lead most of the operational structure during her time at Medpoint.

She left Medpoint in August 2018 to finally pursue her dream of law school.

AROUND THE WORLD IN TWENTY-EIGHT DAYS

As the company rapidly expanded to sites and projects around the world, it required me to travel and monitor our team of over one hundred folks around the United States, Canada, Europe, and Asia. The travel gave me the unique opportunity to see places and meet clients and contacts I never thought I would have the chance to meet.

The most memorable of these trips came in the fall of 2013. It was a journey of twenty-eight days, fourteen flights, and twenty-four thousand miles—I flew literally around the world. After a smooth flight from Greenville to New York, I boarded my first-ever business flight to London. I was fifty years old.

Meetings went well in London, and I took the train over for my first client visit in Wales. It was there, over dinner with friends, that I learned for the first time that the Brits enjoyed a slightly different definition for the word *shagging*. It certainly did not mean dancing.

The next leg took me to the beautiful city of Amsterdam, one of the prettiest cities I've ever experienced. After meeting with two of our folks there in the region, I decided to visit one of the city's "coffee" shops. Once there, I decided to experiment with legal marijuana. As is normally the case with me, if a little is good, more is better. I asked the lady for a "strong" sample and then headed to the airport for my trip to Malaysia. After taking four "hits" on my new purchase, I felt no impact of the cannabis and found checking in and walking through the airport to be a breeze. Then it hit me.

I was in the business lounge, getting ready for a snack and a glass of wine, when my peripheral vision went from normal to as if I was looking through a straw.

For the next two hours, I experienced paranoia like I've never had in my life.

I was convinced that if I didn't get on the flight to Kuala Lumpur, I would probably die in this very beautiful European city. Again, extreme paranoia.

Fortunately, I did make it onto the plane, and after a short layover in Abu Dhabi, I landed in the capital city of Malaysia, sober and cannabis free. The fourteen-hour flight "high" was over.

The next morning, I had a lunch meeting with one of my clients, a Muslim dad who was a quality-assurance executive from the local area. The lunch stretched into dinner, and we ended up spending ten hours together.

Yes, we took care of business, but my biggest takeaway that day was the freedom and ease with which we discussed faith and family topics. I walked away from him that night encouraged, as I clearly perceived a strong commitment on his part to his family, faith, and work.

Then I had a weekend off in Bangkok. The city offered me everything that makes it famous: great food, unique entertainment, and warm hospitality.

Pat, who used to work for one of my employees, took me all over the heavily populated city for three days. We ate, drank, laughed, and enjoyed some really cool Thai experiences, including local boxing matches. But the afternoon at his Buddhist temple had the biggest impact on me. It was interesting to see my friend worship in a very different setting than the one that I was used to. I admired and respected the sincere pursuit of his beliefs.

Shanghai also gave me an experience of a lifetime. For the first and only time in my life, I was robbed.

After a generous meal from my client in downtown Shanghai, I was on my way back to the hotel when the event happened. With a little bit of time to kill before going to bed for the evening, I wandered into a retail shop that was right off the Shanghai version of Times Square.

Once I was inside the building, the doors were locked, and six rough-looking characters made me sit on the sofa of an interior room of a retail store, where they held me hostage for nearly two hours. I refused to turn over to them what amounted to nine hundred American dollars, or 6219 yuan. As I held my ground and refused to go along with their extortion attempt, they began to disappear one at a time. Sometimes I'm quick on my feet, and sometimes not. But that night, I was razor sharp! Perhaps out of sheer fear.

I told them that my client, a company near Shanghai, knew where I was and would be looking for me to return to the hotel soon. Finally, they bought my bluff and allowed me to exit out the back of the building after I gave them only the sixty dollars I had in my pocket instead of forcing me on the unwanted trip to the ATM. As the guy opened the back door, he grunted, "You are a very smart man." I can't remember what emotion was more dominant to me that night: fear, gratitude, or anger.

IT'S REALLY ABOUT PEOPLE

As the CEO of Medpoint, I've had the opportunity to speak at hundreds of events since starting the company. I've been amazed at the warm reception I've received as a keynote, session, and panel speaker. I feel it's a gift. And it's my desire to exercise that gift as much as possible in the years I have remaining—to make a difference in the lives of individuals and organizations. That recently led me to start the Crumpton Group (ChuckCrumpton.com), a business devoted to public speaking and executive and team coaching/building. My mission with this outreach is to help people and companies become champions.

My life at Medpoint revolves around FDA standards and ISO regulations. But at the end of the day, it's really about people. Among all of the projects we tackle, we do a fantastic job of auditing companies that make up the supply chain for our clients. But I am firmly convinced that the reason we do so well with our deliverables and metrics is that we focus heavily on the people we audit, in addition to the standards and regulations we follow.

More than the trips, sights, and experiences, what brought me the greatest joy at Medpoint have been the folks who have touched my life in some special way. In addition to my incredibly talented, faithful, and loyal employees, led by my trusted friend Rich, the following people have my deepest gratitude. The list is certainly not exhaustive.

- **LARRY H.**—for giving me a shot long before he knew how little I knew about healthcare.

- **MARK B.**—for being patient as we worked through a difficult and imperfect project that helped launch our business.

- **TRACY O.**—for giving me time, care, and technical knowledge that I desperately needed.

- **BOB W.**—for trusting me and always having my back.

- **MYRNA M.**—for being a truly collaborative client and a person / single mom who inspires me personally and professionally more than she'll ever know.

- **MIKE C.**—for always doing what he said he would do. Trust was more valuable than paper.

- **ALEX G.**—for being a shining example of strong and dedicated leadership while never forgetting the basics and important things in life.

- **TRENT W.**—for demonstrating integrity in life and business and just doing it right.

- **SAM K.**—for inspiring me to do the improbable with zeal and enthusiasm and to invite others on that journey.

- **LOU K.**—for raw and unbridled enthusiasm and creativity that has shaped economies and industries.

- **WAYNE F.**—for reminding me that the greatest conversations in life have little to do with the dollar.

Because of these folks and many, many more, the Medpoint of today is so radically different than the Medpoint of May 2002. Yet it is still very much the same. We have grown up and become a multimillion-dollar global company, but our values and principles have never changed.

I am proudest of initiatives we are involved in today:

1. Excellent customer service that exceeds expectations.

2. Allocated monies dedicated to employee personal growth and development.

3. Community involvement as a team and individuals on a regular basis.

4. More charitable donations than ever before, making a difference with organizations like Habitat for Humanity, Ronald McDonald House, Lowcountry Orphan Relief, Wounded Warrior Project, Lunch Buddies, Saint Jude Children's Hospital, single-mom ministries, and others. We have been given so much; we are compelled to give back.

Thank you to the many employees, clients, and associates who have made this incredible ride worth it and possible since the early days of toolshed life.

CHAPTER 8

AT JUST THE RIGHT TIME

Sometimes the best things in life are unplanned.

Former US secretary of state Condoleezza Rice once said, "Life is full of surprises and serendipity. Being open to unexpected turns in the road is an important part of success. If you try to plan every step, you may miss those wonderful twists and turns."

As my divorce decree indicated, the last day of my twenty-eight-year marriage in my home would be April 19. On that same day, 655 miles away, Rana would lose her husband of twenty-six years to a terrible battle with cancer. We had not met yet, but our paths would cross in a most surprising way. Tragedy had struck for both of us—divorce and death. Both are horrible.

Months later, over dinner, Rana and I would discuss these two events with bone-chilling recall to try to fully understand how and why God had orchestrated our friendship.

A year earlier, before my move to Charleston, I had joined my friend Dave at the Pavilion Bar, a rooftop bar in one of Charleston's finest hotels. Kelly and Kyra, a couple from Mount Pleasant, were also there relaxing on that beautiful Saturday afternoon. We talked sports, running, and family stuff for a long time and promised to stay in touch.

Months later, I ran into Kelly and Kyra again, this time at their son's sporting event in Greenville. Again, we had fun and drinks and promised to stay in touch.

Eight months later, I ran into Kyra in front of Stars Restaurant on King Street in downtown Charleston. At first, I didn't recognize her because I was absolutely exhausted after returning from a long trip in California. I was partially in a fog because life was becoming more difficult with the divorce process imminent. I'm a natural extrovert and love going out, but that night I felt like crashing on the sofa and ordering pizza. I managed to shower and change into a pair of dress shorts and a shirt and then head out to meander down King Street for dinner. As I did most days on the way out the door, I paused at my wall of inspiration:

You are free.

It was a steamy hot Saturday night in Charleston with the temperature at ninety degrees and similar humidity. I was spent from the heat and jet lag, when I heard, "Hey, Chuck, it's Kyra."

Snapping back to reality, I said, "Hey, it's good to see you again."

"Chuck, this is my neighbor Rana," Kyra said with a smile and a hug.

"Rana, it's nice to meet you," I said to her and then invited them upstairs to the restaurant for a drink. After a couple of drinks, some laughs, and a few groans about the heat, the three of us headed out to dinner at Halls Chophouse two blocks down the street. As always, we were warmly greeted at the door and ushered to our table in the bar area close to the live jazz band. It turned out to be a beautiful evening of conversation and friendship in spite of the heat and jet lag.

In the ensuing months, as Rana and I got to know each other, I realized we were totally different—from different worlds and different experiences—but we were very much the same people in goals, values, and dreams for our families. We would talk for hours about our fears, struggles, hopes, and past lives. No conversation or topic of any kind was off limits.

Very early into our friendship, I shared details of the darkest and most painful chapters of my life. I wanted nothing to be hidden in the shadows. I wanted to be known—good, bad, and ugly. Living my life transparently had become my new normal. She listened and cared and hung on every word as if it were a best-selling novel. Through the building of this friendship, my very dark world of divorce, discouragement, and disillusionment seemed to come alive with light and hope.

THROUGH SHADOWS, FOG, AND FUNK

Then I made a terrible mistake. Excited about the prospects of introducing Rana to family and friends, I invited her to my first (and only) CrossFit competition in Charleston. It would be brutal, and I needed all the support I could get!

My parents and daughter had made the long trip from their homes in North Carolina and western South Carolina to watch me compete. But I made the mistake of prematurely introducing Rana to my daughter, Katie. The family situation I was working through was too raw for her yet, and in my excitement over this new friendship, I failed to exercise wisdom and patience. That decision would cause pain and separation between my daughter and me for a year—a very long year. I'm so happy that the two of them are now incredibly close, largely due to Rana's unwavering love and patience and Katie's grace and forgiving spirit.

Since our relationship started, Rana has always been there for me in spite of all the baggage I brought into our life. Saddled with sadness, self-diagnosed PTSD, guilt, and stress, I brought toxic behaviors into our friendship—criticalness, anger, impatience, and doubt all combined with an overuse of alcohol to ease the pain and soften the hurt of my failed marriage. She never abandoned me, and she demonstrated incredible patience as the shackles of a messed-up mind and heart began to heal. As I told family and friends many times, Rana loved me the way God loves me, through the shadows, fog, and funk of long, painful days and nights. I remain stunned at her enormous capacity to love and embrace broken people.

In my healing, I began to desire a closer connection with God, but I still had so many questions, questions like, "Does God still love me despite my divorce?" and "Will my friends accept my new normal and my new sweetheart?" I had been burned and rejected by some friends because my lifestyle didn't match theirs, and I didn't want to deal with additional relational pain.

I attended and soon invited Rana to the Alpha group at Saint Andrew's Church. Alpha was a nine-week course on Monday nights that offered a good, hot meal to a group of seven hundred people looking for answers. Topics included major issues of faith, including God, prayer, the Holy Spirit, and others. It was really designed for the unchurched, the unbeliever, the folks who had walked away from their faith. I had studied theology at a high level, and I felt like I knew scripture and history pretty well, but my relationship with God was, at best, stagnant. In the meeting each week, all points of view, all pros and cons of faith and God-related topics were encouraged and welcomed. The large group broke out into smaller groups for discussion. The dialogue each evening of the course was warm, challenging, raw, and inviting. I felt my heart being warmed again.

Our little ragtag breakout group of multichurched people led by Ed and Bev Blanton went on to meet long after the nine-week course had ended. Rana and I still meet monthly for dinner, wine, and study with these loving and kind friends. The fellowship is amazing, the conversation real, and the menu includes some of the best damn food I've ever enjoyed. They have loved us immensely, and I'm grateful for their faithful friendship. As I recently reminded a friend who is struggling with severe depression, people are meant to do life with other people, as nonperfect as it looks. There are many well-meaning, sincere, and loving people who will join us on the journey, if we let them.

> *Through tears, joy, and pain, beautiful friendships are born. They say roses grow best in the manure*

Time is generally an ally in most painful situations. Since I had screwed up earlier by introducing Rana to my daughter, I was scared to death of making the same mistake with my son. Then, one day, my son and I had lunch at Whole Foods while Rana and I were visiting San Diego. After lunch, followed by a deep breath and a long lean back in his chair, my son said, "Dad, I'm ready to meet Rana. If she's going to be in your life, I want to be in hers." Later that night, over dinner and drinks, Charles embraced Rana and would soon accept and love her without reservation. She will never be my kids' mom, nor does she want to assume that title, but she has loved my children unconditionally with a fervor since the day she and I met.

Relationships are tough and messy. Sometimes it just takes time, patience, and prayer to heal and close wounds. My daughter and son have a wonderful relationship with Rana now, but it didn't happen overnight. I don't think it was supposed to, the more I reflect on it. Through tears, joy, and pain, beautiful friendships are born. They say roses grow best in the manure.

On Sunday, July 22, 2018, I was given a rose.

THE RIGHT TIME

Due to crazy, non-orchestrated plans from several family members coming into Charleston, I secretively and craftily planned a backyard party at my house. Since the thirty-five family members were traveling in from all over the country, no one knew that this backyard party was the venue I was going to use to ask Rana to marry me. After eight months of intense shopping, planning, and designing, I would present her with a diamond ring and ask for her hand in marriage. On Thanksgiving Day the year prior, I had asked her mom, Sylvia (one of my favorite people on the planet), for permission to marry her daughter. Sylvia said, "Yes! When?" Sylvia and I have shared some wonderful memories, lots of laughs, loud songs, and a few of my world-famous Bloody Mary's over the past few years. I am blessed to have this spunky, Serbian, eighty-eight-year-old jewel in my life.

I asked my children, who were in town for this "backyard party," to join me for Sunday brunch. No one on earth had seen the ring (other than my jeweler), and no one had a clue I would pop the question that day. I wanted to honor Katie and Charles by telling them of my plans first. As we finished breakfast, they began to talk openly about Rana. For the next hour they would rattle through a list of reasons why they loved her and were happy to see us together. It was unsolicited and very emotional.

When they finished, I reached into my pocket, pulled out the ring, and said, "No one knows this, but this afternoon at five o'clock at the party, I'm going to ask Rana to marry me." I think the servers at the Sweetwater Café thought we were on drugs as the tears flowed uncontrollably down our faces. It was all I could do to contain myself; the next four hours seemed like an eternity.

There was a 70 percent chance of hard rain that afternoon, typical summer thunderstorms in the South. As family began to pour in for the party, I knew it was time, just the right time. I assembled everyone together in my little kitchen, near the sofa where I first told Rana I loved her, and gingerly got down on my knees. I thanked her for her unwavering love and asked her to marry me. She was so shocked she couldn't get any words out. I love my dad's smart-ass sense of humor. He said, "Rana, I don't blame you. Take your time with the answer." She finally composed herself and agreed to be my life partner.

Later, two minutes after everyone loaded into their cars to leave, it started to rain. Tears of joy in my new life had replaced tears of sorrow from my old life.

Rana and I both wanted a small, intimate wedding. After a lot of thought and conversation, we had a plan. We asked our bishop, Rev. Steve Wood of Saint Andrew's Church, to come to our house and perform a very small, private ceremony with just the two of us and our parents. That was December 19, 2018, long since we first met on that hot and humid night on King Street.

We chose that particular date for personal reasons, but getting Steve to the house would be nothing short of a miracle. Steve is the rector of our large congregation and the bishop for thirty-two churches in the Carolinas, representing thousands of parishioners. His travel schedule and responsibilities are enormous. But oddly enough, it was one of the few nights of the year he was available to do our ceremony.

Our parents gathered at our house for communion about thirty minutes prior to us exchanging our vows. It was the first time in my life that I took communion with my parents. It was a sober and special time for the six of us. At just the right time, Rana and I exchanged private, handwritten vows to each other. With the lights of the Christmas tree glistening off the large mirror above the fireplace in the front room of my house, we promised to love each other through the good and the bad, the ups and the downs of life. We had both experienced pain in our prior marriages, and we understood the gravity and the brevity of those words.

We then bolted to Stars Rooftop Bar & Grill, where we joined fifty of our closest family and friends. The celebration was indeed special—eating, drinking, and dancing with the people closest to us. It doesn't get any better.

It's really amazing how our two families from the North and the South have come together so beautifully. In addition to my amazing brother, David, I now have two other dudes whom I call brothers, Sam and David White. They are both badass guys who would have my back in any battle. I am also grateful for the love and closeness of Rana's children, Nick and Mia, two people who are beautiful inside and out. I cherish my time with them, and I'm excited to see what the future holds for them as well as Katie and Charles.

I'm not smart enough to have figured this all out on my own. I'm glad I didn't have to.

AFTERWORD

I hope you enjoyed the book. It turned out to be an easier and less daunting project than I thought going into it. I felt I gained momentum and confidence in the second half of the book. It's never easy to remember details from thirty or forty years ago, but I felt like the better I could remember those intricate details of my life and business, the more interesting my story would be for you.

Writing this book did a lot of things for me. I was encouraged, challenged, and even more inspired to share my gifts to benefit others. It takes a lot of focus and energy to write a book—I felt like a heavyweight boxer at the end of the fight after the close of each chapter. But it was imperative for me to "get it right." To maintain my integrity in this process, it was important for me to choose my words carefully. I trust none of those words were offensive, but what you just read is the real Chuck, and I wanted you to see me, clearly and transparently.

As I reflect back on more than fifty years of recall and memories, I have a few regrets, of course. I could have been better in every area of my life, but there are not many radical changes I would have made. I don't say that out of egotism or extreme narcissism, but truly from a heart full of absolute gratitude. Again, to repeat the words of Dave Ramsey, "I'm better off than I deserve." My life has been full of enormous range: joys, tears, victories, and defeats. I'm in a good place—ready, excited, and hopeful to help others in this second half of my life.

Still, I have to be careful with my enthusiasm—not because I'm a talented writer, but because I have millions of other thoughts to share to help people be champions. It will take diligent thought and discernment, since my priorities in life are being a dialed-in husband to Rana and a great dad to Katie and Charles. There is only so much time we have; you can't ride multiple horses across the finish line.

In this overly digital age, we are overwhelmed with noise, technological barriers to real life, and plastic personas. Yet I believe we are in the embryonic start of a revolution of expression, one in which vulnerability and transparency may be gathering momentum. I can tell you in my own life, being transparent (even with this book) has been hard as hell. There are so many good things that come out of being vulnerable and transparent with others, one of which is trust.

Personally and professionally, I've seen the benefits of being real in my life. When you drop your guard and allow others in and eradicate the bullshit of a protected image, beautiful things happen. People will see the real you, and the real you is amazing.

Consider joining me on our journey, yours and mine, toward transparency and vulnerability. It will be scary, but we can take it one step at a time.

I promise you three things that will happen in the process:

1. You will build trust. Trust will be the foundation to overcome any conflict.

2. You will have less stress. Some things in life just don't matter.

3. You will be astonished at how it affects others.

Thanks for being with me on this journey. If I can help you in any way, please reach out to me at ChuckCrumpton.com.

I would love to hear from you.

Other than my desire for you to embrace transparency and vulnerability, let me leave you with a few takeaways from my life and this book:

1. Let in the people who love and care for you.

2. Life has no perfect trajectory, no matter how hard you try.

3. Pursue new paradigms of life and business.

4. Don't let a "piece" of anything rob you of peace.

5. Chase reconciliation.

6. Stay healthy in the darkness.

7. Good professionals—doctors, lawyers, and CPAs—are worth the price.

8. Look for mental-health warning signs in the people you love.

9. Live the life you love; love the life you live.

10. *The best and most beautiful things in the world cannot be seen or even touched—they must be felt with the heart.*
    —Helen Keller

CPSIA information can be obtained
at www.ICGtesting.com
Printed in the USA
LVHW042353261119
638675LV00018B/733/P